Calling Down the FIRE

Dr. Jimmy D. Pritchard

This book was donated by:
Dr. Jimmy D. Pritchard and
First Baptist Church
PO Box 97
Forney, TX 75126

www.CrossHousePublishing.com

**To order more copies
of *Calling Down the Fire*
Contact:
CrossHouse Publishing
P.O. Box 461592
Garland, Texas 75046**

**CALL: 1-800-747-0738
Fax: 1-888-252-3022
Email: crosshousepublishing@earthlink.net
Visit: www.crosshousepublishing.com**

Copyright Jimmy D. Pritchard, 2005
All Rights Reserved
Printed in the United States of America
by United Graphics, Inc., Mattoon, IL
Cover design by Greg Crull

Unless otherwise noted, all Scripture quotations are taken from Holy Bible, New International Version, copyright 1973, 1978, 1984 by International Bible Society
Library of Congress Control Number: 2005920090
ISBN 0-929292-60-X

ACKNOWLEDGEMENTS

I cannot possibly personally extend thanks to all who have made contributions to the compiling of this book. Someone once asked me what length of time is required to prepare a sermon. After being in the ministry now for a couple of decades, my answer was, "About 20 years." In many ways, this book has been years in the making.

The gracious people of the First Baptist Church of Forney, Texas, comprise one of the finest churches in our land. Their prayers and support of their pastor cannot be measured. Much of this work was completed during a sabbatical my church gave me on my 10th anniversary at the church. Wayne Gaylord transcribed many of my preached messages. These transcripts comprised the foundational material for the book. Rick and Sandra Wilson and Paul and Rudie English provided their "homes away from home" for writing and dreaming.

My wife, Jeannette, and children, James, John, and Julie, have encouraged me along the way. I dedicate this work to them.

Finally, everything is for the glory of Jesus Christ. He is everything.

TABLE OF CONTENTS

Introduction	5
Chapter 1—A Hero of the Faith	7
Chapter 2—Calling Down the Fire	15
Chapter 3—Under a Broom Tree	24
Chapter 4—The Passing of the Mantle: the Call of Elijah	33
Chapter 5—An Incident	42
Chapter 6—Pick Up the Mantle	51
Chapter 7—Ditch Diggers	60
Chapter 8—Bring Me Another Jar	70
Chapter 9—Seven Sneezes	79
Chapter 10—Wild Vines	88
Chapter 11—Take a Dip	101
Chapter 12—When the Iron Swims	112
Chapter 13—Opened Eyes	123
Chapter 14—A Living Legacy	134

INTRODUCTION

Our days are filled with opportunities to share the Good News of Jesus Christ. Many seek to fill the vacuum in their lives that has become evident through the disappointment of failed promises of secularism, materialism, and hedonism. In days like these in biblical times as well as in history, God has provided someone who could call down the fire of heaven. As record numbers of people have sought a touch from God for their hurting hearts, too often they have sought their answer at church and found a cold pulpit rather than fire from heaven.

In our culture, we have lost the primacy of the pulpit. Proverbs 29:18 declares, "Where there is no revelation, the people cast off restraint." We witness a total lack of restraint in our society because no one pays attention to a word from God. He is speaking, but few are listening.

In the days of Elijah and Elisha, the same conditions existed. God spoke through these men in such a way that they had to be heard. The people had to reject or accept the fire from heaven. Ignoring it was impossible.

Fire yet to be called from heaven still exists. James and John asked the Lord if they should call down some of this fire on the Samaritans who had rejected the Lord Jesus Christ. Though denied by our Lord, He did not say no fire was available. Later, the fire of God did fall on these Samaritans in the form of a great spiritual awakening!

I am convicted that the God of Elijah has some fire for us in our day. Don't ask the question, "Where is the God of Elijah", but rather ask, "Where are the Elijahs of God?"

I cannot possibly give credit to the sources used in this work. They are derived from notes in my files from messages, articles, books, and personal study of the Word of God. I claim little originality but am obligated to those God has used to call down the fire from heaven into my life.

The desire of my heart in this work is to make a plea for a generation of God's people to stand in fear of no one but God. I plea that they will know nothing but Jesus Christ and Him crucified and pay whatever price is necessary to call down the fire from heaven, restore the primacy of our pulpits, and be used by God to usher in a time of spiritual awakening.

God, send us those who, once again, can call down the fire!

Dr. Jimmy D. Pritchard

Chapter 1

A HERO OF THE FAITH

1 Kings 17:1-24

We live in a day of hero worship. The problem is that few exist who exhibit heroic character or qualities. As you read through the New Testament, you find scattered references to a great hero of the faith. This hero is the Old Testament prophet Elijah. He is referenced not as "a" prophet but as "the" prophet. We learn, grow, are challenged and are blessed as we study about heroes of the faith. We especially are blessed when we study Elijah—the John Wayne of preachers—and his successor, Elisha.

Elijah is a fearless, strong man of faith and a man of God. His life and ministry elicit awe and inspiration. Much can be learned of him from his legacy.

"See, I will send you the prophet Elijah before that great and dreadful day of the Lord comes" (Mal. 4:5).

His life is so great that he is connected to the promise of the Messiah's arrival. The Lord Jesus Christ speaks of Elijah. He explains his role and spirit in relation to John the Baptist,

"For all the prophets and the Law prophesied until John. And if you are willing to accept it, he is the Elijah who was to come" (Matt. 11:13-14).

The forerunner of Jesus Christ, John the Baptist, the man of the wilderness who preached repentance, saying "make way for the coming of the Lord", does so in the spirit of Elijah. On the mount of Transfiguration, when Jesus Christ is shown in His glory, Elijah along with Moses stand beside Him. Elijah casts one of the longest shadows of any Old Testament preacher. With a legacy such as this, his life and message are crucial for us as we seek to live as ambassadors for Christ.

During Elijah's life and ministry a battle has been joined for the very soul of the nation of Israel. The chosen people are in the process of rejecting the faith of their fathers. Their attitude would have fit in perfectly today. Their ideas of tolerance mirror the politically correct philosophies of our day. Ahab, the King of Israel, along with his wife, Jezebel, is a champion for the new tolerance of their day. They worship Baal, the god of the storm. Though they persecute those who worshiped the God of Abraham, Isaac, and Jacob, they allow it to continue. The rub begins when those who worship Jehovah proclaim all others gods to be false idols with no power. The rancor of the king is expressed by the intolerance and audacity of a man like Elijah, who would dare proclaim that Jehovah was the only true God. The country is in turmoil. The people are torn between the God of their fathers and this new way.

At this time God sends a hero. He sends a man who is not aspiring to be politically correct but to be biblically correct. That is what makes Elijah so great. His great aim is not political correctness but biblical correctness. He steps into the battle with no credentials or introduction. He speaks only words that are accompanied by the power of the living God. He is one of the heroes of our faith. He can call down the fire from heaven. In our day of spiritual drought, how great is our need for those with the spirit of Elijah to begin again to call down the fire! Our pulpits have lost their primacy because they have lost the fire. Would that God would raise up a generation of those who would dare call down the fire again! Note how Elijah's ministry begins.

AN UNANNOUNCED APPEARANCE

Elijah just shows up. Nothing in the Bible introduces him; we have no background information. The Bible simply says, "Elijah the Tishbite . . . says . . .." Where was he from? Scholars and archaeologists cannot find his hometown. He grew up in anonymity. Who knows what schools God had put him through out there in the lonely days being by himself developing his relationship with the Lord? His name means "Yahweh (the Old Testament name for God) is my God." He simply appears unannounced and unheralded and proclaims, "Though you do not know who I am, and you probably never heard of me, I want to tell you something. Until I say so, God is not going to let it rain. Then we will see what Baal, the god of the storm, thinks about that." All who hear him surely believe he is unbalanced at best and demented at worst. Rain does not fall for a week, then a month, then a year, and then for more than two years. The words of this man of God are accompanied by the power of God.

This unknown, unannounced man appears and through his words shuts the heavens. The King's god, Baal, is the god of the storm. When the storm arrives, it is accompanied by rain. Elijah directs a frontal assault on the false god of the politically correct pundits of his day. God's hero takes a great risk in his stand. If rain falls, his credibility will be gone. His confidence is revealed in that he speaks the word of God. The passage says, "As the Lord, God of Israel, lives, whom I serve" (NIV) is translated "before whom I stand" (NASB) in another translation. It is a picture of Elijah standing in the very council room of Almighty God. As he waits to serve, God gives him his assignment. Elijah is simply repeating what He has heard from God. The risk is not his but God's. Anytime we take our stand and hold our Scriptural convictions, we are not tested, but the God who has spoken is responsible. None of His words ever fall to the ground without accomplishing their purpose. A risk of faith always exists when we take our stand and say, "Here's what God says. Here's where I'm going to stand." That is what spiritual heroes do. They throw everything they have and everything they are on the line in order to obey what God lays on their heart.

Elijah has developed and nurtured this special relationship with God in a quiet place—in a secret place where no public eye has been on him. In that secret place, he becomes not "a" prophet but "the" prophet. The same is true today. The pulpit in the public view doesn't make the prophet. In the solitude and the quiet place and the secret place and in the place of anonymity God grows and develops the prophet. He has no resume or letter of recommendation. A life grown in the holy place—in the council of God—is where a man gets the fire. Power accompanies the proclamation of what is heard when standing in the council of God. The hero stands to proclaim a word from God. That word always is true to Scripture and applicable to life.

We still have spiritual heroes. Their qualities mirror Elijah's. Our heroes are obedient. They do things simply because God desires it. They are patient. Elijah is by himself. His relationship with God is enough. He is fearless. He fears no one, though he does have a brief lapse. He is faithful. But the thing about Elijah that gives us great hope is that he is a common, ordinary person just like you and me.

"The prayer of a righteous man is powerful and effective. Elijah was a man just like us. He prayed earnestly that it would not rain, and it did not rain on the land for three and a half years. Again he prayed, and the heavens gave rain, and the earth produced its crops" (Jas. 5:16b-18).

Imagine that—a person like us. If God can do such exploits with Elijah, He can do them through us.

God has many men and women serving Him in the anonymous arenas of life. They may believe that no one is noticing. They are in the secret place with Him, nurturing their relationship. They are in our cities and towns. They stay in the council of God. They faithfully proclaim the Word of God. They are pastors and laypersons who love the Lord Jesus Christ. Yet none can call down the fire.

In recent years, God has given the churches the ear of our nation. During the Gulf War people, seeking a word from heaven, flocked to the churches. After 9/11 people in great masses sought a word from God. The churches were full. I don't know what they heard, but they did not see the fire of God. Who knows how many opportunities we will have to speak the Word of God to such an eager audience? The disciples are given three opportunities to stand with their Lord through prayer in the Garden of Gethsemane. We have had two opportunities to catch the ear of our nation. At neither time did we answer the call. That is why a study of Elisha and Elijah is so appropriate. If ever the time was right, now is when we need to call down the fire.

AN UNUSUAL REQUEST

His assault on the King's god brings repercussions. Ahab wants him dead. God sends Elijah to safety at the Kerith

Ravine. God sends him to an isolated place where a little stream will provide water for him during the drought. The ravens bring him food. In the morning, the blackbirds bring food. He eats the food and drinks from the stream. No one knows what he does the rest of the day. He is all by himself. Nobody knows where he is. Sometimes walking with God is a lonely life. Sometimes the follower of Christ is left out when others say, "Everybody is doing it." This may appear to be lonely, but it is anything but, since God is with him.

The little brook finally dries up. God gives another unusual request. He tells Elijah to go to a certain town where God has prepared a widow to meet his needs. When he arrives, the widow declares that she is cursed and about to die. She is preparing the last meal for herself and her son. Elijah encourages her to go ahead and prepare the meal but to give him a part of it first. She complies; from this act of obedience flows a great miracle, as they did not run out of food throughout the drought.

Note the sovereignty of God. When God commands Elijah to go to the widow's town, she has no idea she is in God's plan. Neither does Elijah. God always has the big picture in view. None of us need understand; we simply need to trust Him. We all need to keep gathering our little sticks in our lives.

We never know what God has commanded on our behalf that is waiting for us around the next corner. What a contrast when you are living in your little world, thinking that God does not know anything about you and does not care anything about your situation, while in heaven God has issued a command with your name on it. You remain faithful; no one knows what kind of miracle God has in store for you.

A UNIQUE OPPORTUNITY

The widow trusts Elijah. She trusts Elijah's God. She trusts what He says. Though some have misplaced that trust, we once again can learn to trust what the preacher says. Our preachers must be truthful to the Lord Jesus Christ. Heroes always are. People will trust the heroes. This widow has a unique opportunity to make a difference in the life of Elijah and in the life of this nation. She begins the day thinking that all she can do is gather sticks and die. Before the day ends, her needs are completely met because of her obedience to the word and will of God. Seemingly, because of that obedience, she will enjoy the blessings of God. His blessings arrive wrapped in a strange package, but this offers her a unique opportunity to experience a great miracle of God.

"Some time later the son of the woman who owned the house became ill. He grew worse and worse, and finally stopped breathing. She said to Elijah, 'What do you have against me, man of God? Did you come to remind me of my sin and kill my son?'" (1 Kings 17:17-18).

This widow already feels cursed because her husband has died and now her son is dead. She has done what God has asked and has honored God's prophet. Now this has happened. God seemingly has repaid her good with evil.

Everyone has been at this place. At times we believe that all obedience has been to no avail. Heaven seems silent; life is the worse for having trusted God. Things may seem that way for a while, but time proves that it is not the case. When life is darkest, God gave a glorious miracle. Elijah takes the boy into his room, prays over him, lies down on him, and the boy's life returns. This is an unforeseen blessing—a unique opportunity to experience the power of God. That power is not experienced from the mountaintop but from the valley.

The widow learns that God can be trusted. She can trust Him then. Can you trust Him now? Can you trust Him in making that proclamation? Can you trust Him as you gather a few little sticks? You find the answer the same way Elijah did. You find it the same way the widow woman did. You obey Him. You may not know why; you likely will not even know the details, but you can rest in knowing that God does know. He has never made a mistake. He will not make His first one with you.

God tells Elijah to go "there" to the Kerith Ravine. "There" He has provided water and food. If Elijah had not gone "there", he would have missed the miracle. He then tells Elijah to go to that little town of Sidon, because "there" He had provided a widow to meet his needs. If Elijah had not gone "there", he would have missed the miracle. When God sends you "there", be assured He has gone before you and has provided all you need. You must go "there", or you will miss it. Are you "there?"

God's plans are wonderful when we are "there" in the center of His will. Let us do what we can to get "there", where we will discover God's power, presence, provision, and purpose. Those who can call down the fire are "there."

Chapter 2

CALLING DOWN THE FIRE

1 Kings 18

First Kings 18 describes one of the greatest spiritual awakenings recorded in the Bible. When God's Spirit does a great work—whether this occurs in a brief season of revival or in an extended time of spiritual awakening—though He needs no assistance, He always has chosen someone to step to the plate in faith, obedience, and purity of heart to spearhead the movement. That is precisely what He does in this great chapter. Elisha calls down the fire.

In I Kings 17 Elijah just shows up one day and proclaims God's message. He says, "At my command, it's not going to rain!" This presents a direct challenge to the politically correct and trendy god of the times, Baal—the god of the storm and of rain and the harvest. No one takes Elijah seriously, but by now more than two years have passed. Rain has not fallen. King Ahab has conducted a search for Elijah, even traveling to other countries and kingdoms. Desperation is beginning to set in.

Some will say that the key to spiritual awakening is prayer. That is correct, but the prayer that moves the hand of God in spiritual awakening and revival is prayer that is born out of desperation. We are experiencing little in the way of spiritual awakening in our day, because few prayers born of desperation are ascending to heaven's throne.

Elijah has been hidden and protected by God during these years of drought. He has spent some time at the Brook Kerith and then in a little town called Sidon. The time has arrived for a contest of the gods. Here are the combatants.

Baal, the god of the storm, is the official god of the king, Ahab, and his queen, Jezebel. On his side in the contest are 450 prophets. Baal's female companion god is called Asherah. She has 400 prophets in her corner. Often the Old Testament refers to Asherah poles that are used in idol worship. Asherah is the goddess of fertility. These poles are carved in the shape of male genitalia. As worshipers gather to worship around these poles, male and female prostitutes are available to assist in worship. So as Baal and Asherah are worshiped, boys and girls are available for worshipers to engage in sexual activities. Our society continues to worship the god of fertility, although we do so in different forms.

The other contestant is Almighty God, the God of Abraham, Isaac, and Jacob. He is the One to whom Israel has made its commitments. God retains a quiet remnant. Though persecuted, it is still faithful. Its champion is the prophet Elijah.

Through the drought, God attains the attention of Ahab and Jezebel. Elijah now makes himself known and issues a challenge to the false gods and their champions. The contest will be held on Mt. Carmel. Elijah lays out the ground rules. Each group will be allowed to prepare a sacrifice and offer worship to its god. The criteria by which to declare the winner will be determined by which god answers by fire.

Just before the contest, Elijah goes before the people and says,

"How long will you waver between two opinions? If the

Lord is God, follow Him, but if Baal is God, follow Him. But the people said nothing" (1 Kings 18:21).

Elijah stands there a lonely man, a hero, and a champion. His heart is broken, but it is burning at the same time. That is the substance of good preaching. When a man of God proclaims a message from God with brokenness and burning, with conviction and compassion, and with persuasion and passion, it will move the heart. Elijah is calling for a decision. The people are hedging a little bit. They would rather not insult the King by rejecting his god, but arguing against a two-year drought is difficult. They decide not to answer at all—not a word. That scenario is repeated all over Christendom Sunday by Sunday as God's preachers call for decision but are answered with not a word. We need desperation that drives to a verdict.

A PROCEDURE RECITED

Elijah offers the prophets of Baal the opportunity to begin. They proceeded with sincere hearts. They have an order of worship. They get the altar together. They make a sacrifice on that altar. They offer their prayers. They have a very good, solid ritual. They have a bulletin with everything laid out. And they are very sincere. They are politically correct. One can almost imagine some in the crowd thinking and sharing how all roads must lead to the same place, that a good life and sincerity in convictions must be all that is required. These are the first politically correct worshipers that can be a model for modern-day secularists.

Though sincere, they are wrong. Sincerity does not and cannot substitute for truth. Even with sincere hearts they face a silent heaven. Midday passes; they continued their frantic prophesying until the time for the evening sacrifice, but no response is heard. No one answers; no one pays attention. With all sincerity and order, they stand before a silent heaven.

Elijah watches while he sits under a tree. He seems to enjoy this very much. He encourages them by suggesting they yell a little louder. Perhaps Baal is asleep and needs to be awakened. He may be on a journey; perhaps he is busy. No answer arrives. When you face a crisis in your life, you do not wish who or whatever you have worshiped to remain silent. Call the front office of your favorite sports team; surely they will send someone over to help you with that rebellious teenager or to solve your marriage or financial problems. Too many are worshiping a politically correct god in an orderly, sincere way, but when you need a supernatural touch from heaven, you stand before a silent heaven.

Many churches and many church leaders fit better with Ahab's crew than with God's champions. They have long since lost the power of God. All that is left is the ritual. They cling to it with all their power. In many churches when the ritual is changed, the people get upset, because ritual is all they have left—ritual without power, sincerity without truth. Everything is in perfect order, but the fire is missing. Few notice that none are added to the kingdom. The fact that ministries are starving for finances does not matter. Many churches have substituted the Great Commission for the Great Convenience. They have become just like these worshipers of Baal and Asherah. Even though they have sincere hearts, they worship before a silent heaven. What we need is a fresh touch from Jesus Christ in our lives. We need a spiritual awakening patterned after what God brings through Elijah. We need somebody to call down the fire.

A POWER REVEALED

Elijah now steps up to bat. Baal and Asherah are unable to answer by fire. Elijah first repairs the altar of God. An altar already exists on Mt. Carmel. It has been used previously to worship God. It now is in disrepair due to neglect. The stones in the altar are scattered, weeds are growing up in the altar, and it is overrun by nonuse. One wonders about the condition of the altar of God in the hearts of people today. The secret place for true fellowship with God is overrun with concerns of the world and with every kind of action and attitude one can imagine. The face of God and the purposes of God and the true worship of God have been absent for so long that the altar within you is in great need of repair. Elijah repaired the altar. He got it ready to be used for that which it was designed. That deep place within each of us is designed to behold the face of God and worship Him. To experience the fire of God, one must repair that altar within.

Many churches need to repair the altar. Over the course of the years, God's intended purpose for the church has been forgotten and thus neglected. The energy of this kind of church is inward and usually can be identified through power groups, criticism, and little if any growth. God's intent—making disciples for His kingdom—is abdicated and ignored. For the fire of God to fall, our churches must repair the altar. We must rediscover God's purpose. When God finds a church that is committed to the Great Commission, His blessings will be evident. The fire will fall.

Secondly, Elijah renews the promises of God. He takes 12 stones and arranges them on the altar. Each stone represents one of the family tribes of Israel to whom God previously has given all of his promises. He gathers together all of these stones, lays them carefully on the newly repaired altar, and recalls the promises of God. Anytime spiritual awakening occurs in a life or in a church, the promises of God are remembered and renewed.

"For no matter how many promises God has made, they are 'Yes' in Christ" (2 Cor. 1:20a).

God has been good to all of His people. Though we have a tendency at times to neglect Him and move away from Him, His promises are true for all times and all seasons. They do not depend on our faith but on the One who gave them. God's promises are as good and as true as God's character. When we renew them and believe them, the fire will fall.

Next, Elijah recalls the word of God. This time of the evening sacrifice is a time the Old Testament law appointed for worship to occur. When the time arrives, worship begins. The Lord God has chosen this nation of Israel. He brings them to their own country. This fulfills the promise He has given Abraham. Now they are in total disarray, as they violently oppose God's purposes for them. On this day, the time arrives for worship. Behold, rising before the Lord Almighty, at the appointed time, is true worship. It has been absent for so long. Now one is worshiping the true God in the ancient true ways. Only one. Elijah is leading, but it is true worship, just like the Word prescribes. God sees one man with a pure heart willing to be obedient. It moves the very heart and hand of God! How we need a few more in Elijah's spirit who will have the courage to repair the altar, renew the promises, and recall the Word of God.

Will you be one of those? Somebody must call down the fire!

Our world, churches, and lives will not experience spiritual awakening apart from our obedience to the Word of God. A recent Barna survey of church members across America discovered that only eight percent agree with this statement:

Faith is important in our lives; we believe we have a responsibility to witness to non-believers; we believe in the existence of a literal person as Savior; we believe that salvation is available only through God's grace and not good deeds; we believe that Jesus Christ lived a simple life; we describe God as the all-knowing, all-powerful Deity who created the universe and still rules it today.

If only eight percent of the members of churches in America believe that, one wonders what the other 92 percent believe, if anything. That same survey revealed that 41 percent would describe themselves as "born again." Those who believe in the total accuracy of the Bible came in at 41 percent also. Many of those who say they believe the Bible obviously do not know what it teaches if only eight percent ascribe to the statement above.

We live in a day when the Bible is under attack and the very heart of Christianity is under attack. Often the attacks originate in churches! Don't expect to experience the fire of God in your life if you are not willing to recall the Word of God and accept it for what it is.

Elijah's worship consists of repairing God's altar, renewing God's promises, and recalling God's Word. Worship does not end at that point. It is just beginning. The true God answers by fire. When the fire falls, the power is revealed. The will of God contains great repentance. A change occurs. Whereas the people do not want to answer a word earlier, they now are eager to proclaim the Lord as God.

Though barbaric, yet as evidence of their commitment, they gathered up these 400 prophets of Baal, take them down to the valley, and kill every one of them. Repentance simply involves a change of direction. It is turning from where we are to where God is. Notice the revival and fire of God is not something Elijah works up, but it is something that God brings down. Repentance and the fire of God cannot be separated.

God's people need to reach the point of desperation so that our prayers bring a burning into our lives of real spiritual strength and renewal. If a time when God needed to reveal Himself in fire and power ever occurred, it is in this day. Though the names have changed, worship of the sensual gods of which Baal and Asherah represent has spread across our land. In some pulpits and incredibly even in some denominational leadership positions are those who proudly flaunt their homosexuality. They proclaim that God has changed His mind on issues such as these.

The politically correct and socially flawed ideas of tolerance proclaim that all truths are equally valid and that any position that claims absolute truth must be silenced. They say everybody is right and that all claims to truth, no matter how divergent, are equally valid. Such is the case in Elijah's day. He puts God's truth into the public forum. The message of the true God prevails. He never has lost a contest and never will.

Continue to put God's truth into the public forum. Ridicule may occur, but God yet may reveal Himself again by fire. May the preachers continue to stand firm and speak boldly! The clarion call must be issued from a repaired altar, a renewed promise, and a recalled word, "Choose you this day whom you will serve!" Though many will answer with "not a word", God will keep to Himself a remnant that will continue to proclaim, "the Lord, He is God!" May you be counted among them. May we again experience a day when the fire falls.

The greatest need in America is for our pulpits to be aflame with the fire of God. An old story tells of a time when the local church building caught on fire in a small, rural town. A bucket brigade was passing the water in buckets to throw on the fire. The preacher found himself in line beside the town atheist. He said, "I've never seen you at church before", to which the atheist replied, "I've never seen the church on fire before!" May God touch the hearts of our pastors. May a generation of men arise who fear nothing but the Lord Jesus Christ, believe the Bible, and have the audacity to call fire down from heaven. When the fire falls, many will arrive to watch it burn. Many will be caught up in the flame. God, send down the fire!

Chapter 3

UNDER A BROOM TREE

1 Kings 19:1-8

Life sometimes can take an unexpected turn. One phone call, one email, or one conversation can change your life forever. Such a change occurs to Elijah. If we are not careful, we can find ourselves as he did, sitting under a broom tree. I recently was asked the questions, "Where do you think you'll be in 10 years? What do you see your life in 10 years?" I just laughed and said, "I have no idea. I don't have any plans." I learned a long time ago that if you want to give God a good laugh, tell Him your plans. You aren't wrong to have plans and desires to bring glory to God in specific ways in your life, but sometimes you are better off simply following Him along as He leads, because you never know what He is bringing around the next corner.

Following a great spiritual awakening in which Elijah is the point man, life takes an unexpected turn. He finds himself brooding, depressed, and dejected as he sits under a broom tree. After his unexpected and unannounced appearance on the scene in Israel, he now has become known as the most powerful prophet in the land. The great revival on Mt. Carmel has brought the nation back to its spiritual roots. How we pray that God might do it again in our day! Perhaps an Elijah is yet among us that will make an unannounced and unexpected appearance soon. How we pray that God will bring spiritual awakening that would magnify Jesus Christ and pale the glory of Mt. Carmel!

We naturally assume that Elijah's ministry is about to rise to unbelievable heights. Had he lived in our day, invitations would flow in to speak at conferences on spiritual awakening and on the secrets of calling down fire from heaven. Elijah has the ear of the entire nation. The time has arrived to print some brochures. For a nominal fee he can arrive to tell the story of the revival on Mt. Carmel. He can ride the wave of momentum and the national publicity into a glorious future and greater ministry.

However, that is not the case. Instead of standing tall and moving forward to greater adventures and victories, Elijah runs into the desert and withdraws under a broom tree. In some versions of the Bible you might read that it is called a juniper tree. It really is a small bush that grows in the desert, does not produce much foliage, and gives no real protection from the sun. Perhaps it is like the small, Texas mesquite tree. The Bible describes his experience:

"Now Ahab told Jezebel everything Elijah had done and how he had killed all the prophets with the sword. So Jezebel sent a messenger to Elijah to say, 'May the gods deal with me, be it ever so severely, if by this time tomorrow I do not make your life like that of one of them.' Elijah was afraid and ran for his life. When he came to Beersheba in Judah, he left his servant there, while he himself went a day's journey into the desert. He came to a broom tree, sat down under it and prayed that he might die. 'I have had enough, Lord,' he said. 'Take my life; I am no better than my ancestors.' Then he lay down under the tree and fell asleep. All at once an angel touched him and said, 'Get up and eat.' He looked around. There by his head was a cake of bread baked over hot coals, and a jar of water. He ate and drank and then lay down again. The angel of the Lord came back a second time and touched him and said, 'Get up and eat, for the journey is too much for you.' So he got up and ate and drank. Strengthened by that food, he traveled forty days and forty nights until he reached Horeb, the mountain of God. There he went into a cave and spent the night. And the word of the Lord came to him: 'What are you doing here, Elijah?' He replied, 'I have been very zealous for the Lord God Almighty. The Israelites have rejected your covenant, broken down your altars, and put your prophets to death with the sword. I am the only one left, and now they are trying to kill me too.' The Lord said, 'Go out and stand on the mountain in the presence of the Lord, for the Lord is about to pass by.' Then a great and powerful wind tore the mountains apart and shattered the rocks before the Lord, but the Lord was not in the wind. After the wind was an earthquake, but the Lord was not in the earthquake. After the earthquake came a fire, but the Lord was not in the fire. After the fire came a gentle whisper. [Still small voice.] When Elijah heard it, he pulled his cloak over his face and went out and stood at the mouth of the cave. Then a voice said to him, 'What are you doing here, Elijah?' He replied, 'I have been very zealous for the Lord God Almighty. The Israelites have rejected your covenant, broken down your altars, and put your prophets to death with the sword. I am the only one left, and now they are trying to kill me too.' The Lord said to him, 'Go back the way you came, and go to the desert of Damascus. When you get there, anoint Hazael king over Aram. Also, anoint Jehu son of Nimshi king over Israel, and anoint Elisha son of Shaphat from Abel Meholah to succeed you as prophet. Jehu will put to death any who escape the sword of Hazael, and Elisha will put to death any who escape the sword of Jehu. Yet I reserve seven thousand in Israel—all whose knees have not bowed down to Baal and all whose mouths have not kissed him.'" (1 Kings 19:1-18).

So on the heels of this tremendous spiritual awakening, Elijah falls into a pit and is joined by three friends called depression, disillusionment, and discouragement. This reaches the point at which he is ready to die. Others have frequented this pit. King David spent a period of time there, as did the Apostle Paul. I believe that even Jesus Christ at certain times in His ministry passed through that same pit.

Historically, some great men who have done great things have spent time in this pit, under a broom tree. Winston Churchill, the great statesman and hero, was prone to long segments of dark depression. Charles Spurgeon, pastor of the first mega-church to ever exist, had deep seasons of depression—under a broom tree. Some of you are there now. Though your life is good and blessed, still you are sitting under the broom tree. Great lessons from the great prophet are under the little tree.

A SPECIFIC TARGET

If you are under a broom tree, you have become a specific target. Everyone who is making a difference for God will become a specific target of Satan. Only Elijah has received a threat from Jezebel. He is the one God is using in a mighty way. In our lives every step of progress and sign of victory will be challenged by Satan. All those on the front line of spiritual warfare will face the challenges of the enemy. Pastors, soulwinners, and prayer warriors are specific targets of Satan because of their impact on the kingdom of darkness. Any time a person's life and ministry begins to impact others for Christ, a bull's eye is placed on them. They become targets and potential broom-tree residents.

Many of my peers have been picked off by the fiery darts of the evil one. Almost weekly I hear of pastors losing the ministry to which God has entrusted them. This is sometimes due to moral issues, sometimes due to burnout, sometimes because of conflict in the church. The greater challenge always accompanies the greater opportunity. As Paul discovers in Ephesus, "because a great door for effective work has opened to me, and there are many who oppose me" (1 Cor. 16:9). Pray for those in your life who are on the front lines of spiritual warfare. Enlist people to pray for you as you engage in battle. Put on the spiritual armor including the shield of faith to put out these fiery darts of Satan that are aimed at specific targets.

Elijah has just stood fearlessly before King Ahab and 400 hostile prophets and been a champion. Now he is running in fear because of a rumor! Queen Jezebel says, possibly just off the cuff, "I'm going to get Elijah." When he hears the rumor, the champion of God cowers down in fear and runs into the desert under a broom tree. "Take my life, Lord, I've had all of this I want." Sometimes life takes a strange turn; we can find ourselves under a broom tree.

Even in the best of lives, circumstances can get difficult. Setbacks occur in careers. The plan that you make for your life—your 10-year plan—does not happen. Work for the Lord is negated, pressure occurs—perhaps through rumors—as Satan attempts to escort you to visit his friends of depression, discouragement, and disillusion under the broom tree. You become a special target.

A SAD TALE

Elijah's broom-tree experience indeed is a sad tale. Elijah is going it alone! The pressure of going it alone finally builds to the point at which he simply cannot take it any longer. His ministry and the resulting drought brings a lot of pain on a lot of people. He has pressure on his life with no one to talk to or pray with. He has lived alone at the brook Kerith. He has been alone with that widow and her son. He stands alone against the false prophets. By his word the drought could have ended, but God is not ready for him to issue that word. Elijah is feeling intense pressure and finally retreats to the broom tree.

This going it alone bears fruit in his life and escorts him to the broom tree, where he sits and says, "I'm worn out." We begin on the path to the broom tree by entering through the door of loneliness. Accompanying us is a sense of being overwhelmed with the challenges of life, a sense of isolation, no sense of respect from peers, a feeling of worthlessness, and a loss of self-confidence. Elijah needs a support system.

All of us need a support system that will be there during the moments that we are sliding toward our broom tree. We need someone who can put his or her arms around us and say, "It's going to be fine; it's going to be all right."

Our church is relocating to a larger site. Early in the process we were putting together all of the plans. Our church had voted to do it, but still, quite a few people were not too certain about it all. After one of the discussions one of our men came up to me and said, "Bro. Jim, I really don't know what we need to do. But, I want you to know, I'm standing with you." I can't tell you how much that meant to me. That was just like putting steel in my bones.

Don't try to go it alone. John Wayne could do it, but that was in the movies. Alone you inevitably will end up under a broom tree. Develop a support group. Pray for each other. Encourage each other. It will keep you out from under a broom tree. It will keep your life from becoming a sad tale.

A SPECIAL TREATMENT

God always gives those He loves a special treatment when we need it the most. Elijah runs away, but he runs right into the Lord. The last place he expects to find God is under the broom tree. Have you ever noticed that when you run away from the Lord, with the next step you run right into Him? The Lord very calmly asks, "What's going on, Elijah?" I see that as a very tender question. Elijah is exhausted. God prescribes some R & R—eat and sleep. After he wakes, God says, "Eat and sleep some more." Amazing what a little bit of rest and healthy diet can do for your perspective! It helps Elijah, as it does us, to get balanced. When we are balanced, we get into a position to hear from God. Elijah is sent to Mt. Horeb, the mountain of God. If that sounds familiar, that's the same place where Moses sees the burning bush. Elijah goes where God is. The special treatment for Elijah under the broom tree: get your physical life balanced, diet and rest, and then go to a place where you can hear from God.

In our stressful world, marriages can be saved, lives enriched, and problems placed in proper perspective if we will follow this prescription for God's special treatment. Get balanced physically; find the place where God is. Our lives are stressed and rushed; the relationships are so shallow, we become susceptible to this broom-tree syndrome. What we need is a little bit of special treatment to get out from under it. God has a special treatment for all of us.

A SURE TRUTH

The only place to find A Sure Truth is in the Word of God. Discovering the presence of God and receiving a Word from Him will bring you out from under that broom tree. Elijah realizes that he does not need to experience the blessings of God. He already has the blessings of God. He has prayed for no rain; a drought has occurred. He asks for rain; it arrives. He has raised a dead child to life. He has the blessings of God. He has to learn that the blessings of God are good, but they will not suffice for our lives. What he needs is not God's blessings but His presence. When we recognize His presence in our lives through Jesus Christ, all blessings are secondary. The presence of God in our lives, not the blessings that take us out from under the broom tree, is what matters.

To answer God's question, "What are you doing here, Elijah?" I paraphrase Elijah's response, "Lord, I feel as though I'm here all by myself. And I've worked so hard, and I've been obedient, but I am so empty, and I am so tired. I'm just ready to cash in."

God answers him with His presence—a mighty wind, wind strong enough to shatter rocks! That's more than a Texas twister. But God is not in the wind. Then an earthquake arrives. The earth moves! That's still not where he finds God's presence. Then appears a fire as you might expect since this is where the burning bush was, but no, God is not in the fire.

Then occurs that gentle blowing. I love how the King James says it—"Still small voice." That's where we hear from God. Not in the thunder and the lightening and the big show, but when the Holy Spirit just reaches into your life and God speaks. I'll tell you that is what will get you out from under the broom tree—the sweet, gentle presence of the Holy Spirit in your life.

When He expresses His presence, He then adds some specifics. His message to Elijah is, "I'm not through with you. I have more stuff for you to do. I need you to go anoint someone as king. I need you to go anoint this guy and to end your loneliness. I already have prepared you an apprentice whose name is Elisha. You are not going to be alone anymore. And by the way, 7,000 more people in Israel have remained faithful to Me and have not bent their knee to the false god, Baal."

Things are not nearly as bad as they seem, even under a broom tree, but Elijah cannot know that until he gets alone in the presence of God. God uses the broom tree in order for Elijah to see the presence and the power of God in this manner. God is so awesome that even a broom-tree experience can be used to bring glory to Himself in your life.

It's all about perspective. Many years ago, the church I was serving did a pictorial directory. A man was very upset because the portrait of his wife was unacceptable. He said it was the worst picture ever taken of her. Two weeks later his wife suddenly died. As I visited in his home, he was holding that portrait in his hand and said it was the most precious possession that he had. Perspective means everything.

You may be under a broom tree. You have been faithful to Christ, yet here you are. Get some rest. Get in position to hear from God. Do not seek His blessing or His hands. Seek His face. Look for His presence. He will change your perspective. He will give you a new purpose, a new power, and a new perspective. He will walk with you out from under your broom tree.

Chapter 4

THE PASSING OF THE MANTLE

1 Kings 19:19-21

Elijah and Moses. These men are the thunder and lightning of God in the Old Testament. On the Mount of Transfiguration Jesus Christ prepares for His week of passion. He takes three of His Apostles—Peter, James and John—apart to a secluded place. There the Lord Jesus Christ is changed before their very eyes. What the Bible calls the Shekinah Glory of God is shown to these men. They also see Elijah and Moses there. Moses is such a great man of God that in the New Testament anytime he is referenced, he usually is not just referred to as a man but to the Old Testament law. Elijah, the great prophet, oftentimes is equated to the entire prophetic ministry. So you have Elijah and you have Moses—the Law and the Prophets. The book of Revelation tells of two witnesses. One of these two witnesses has the power to shut up the sky so that it will not rain. That seems to be an obvious reference to the great prophet, Elijah. The other witness has the power to turn water into blood and to strike the earth with every kind of plague. This seems to be an obvious reference to the Lawgiver Moses. These great men of God have a lot of similarities. Indeed they are the thunder and lightning of God in the Old Testament.

One of their similarities is that both of them are the mentors of an apprentice. Moses prepares Joshua to take his place. Elijah becomes a mentor to the man who will succeed him. Elisha is to become Elijah's assistant and the heir-apparent to his prophetic ministry. Much can be learned from the mentor/apprentice relationship.

Leading to the passage of the call of Elisha, the Bible records the glory and the pain of Elisha's ministry. He has called down fire from heaven and led in a tremendous victory for God. Following the victory occurs a time of burnout, possibly even depression. The pressure of his ministry takes its toll. One of the ways God speaks to Elijah and ministers to Him is promising Him a successor. Elisha becomes more than just a successor but also a servant and friend. 1 Kings 19:19-21 tells the story.

"So Elijah went from there and found Elisha son of Shaphat. He was plowing with twelve yoke of oxen, and he himself was driving the twelfth pair. Elijah went up to him and threw his cloak around him. Elisha then left his oxen and ran after Elijah. 'Let me kiss my father and mother good-by,' he said, 'and then I will come with you.' 'Go back,' Elijah replied. 'What have I done to you?' So Elisha left him and went back. He took his yoke of oxen and slaughtered them. He burned the plowing equipment to cook the meat and gave it to the people, and they ate. Then he set out to follow Elijah and became his attendant."

God still issues a call today. Many of you reading this have heard the call of God. Whether he calls Adam, Paul, Simon, or Andrew, He always calls us by name. It's that still, small voice that once you hear, you never can be the same. The call is to everyone and is not necessarily connected to a preaching ministry or to a vocational Christian ministry. It is a call to a life; it is extended to everyone who knows Jesus Christ as Savior and Lord. The call can be to any area of life. It is God's purpose for you. A fine, young man—an early apprentice of mine—declared to me that he did not think God was calling him into the ministry, as he had formerly discerned. He believed God wanted him to become an attorney. Doing the right thing and doing what God wants never is wrong. Today that young man is the chief of staff for a United States Senator and actively serves Christ in that position.

THE MOMENT

When the call arrives, it is clear. No mistake occurs when God speaks. Those who have heard God's call on their lives know exactly how clear it is. Elisha's day in our text begins like any other day. By the time the day is over, he has heard a clear call from God. Elisha likely has a healthy relationship with God before this meeting. God knows Elisha's heart already and has great plans for him. God knows that this young man is one of those in Israel who has not bent his knee and kissed the false god, Baal. Elisha has no idea what is about to happen to him, but his life is about to take a drastic turn.

Sometimes God breaks into our lives in unexpected ways and astounds us with His power and purpose. Years ago, during my studies at Southwestern Seminary in Fort Worth, Texas, I attended a chapel service. I did not know who was speaking, but I noticed an old man seated on the platform and heard something about the number of books he had written. I thought the last thing I needed was to hear some old author speak for 20 minutes, so I looked for a way out. The music for the service already had begun, so out of respect, I decided to stay. As the old man slowly made his way to the pulpit, I prepared to go into neutral for a few minutes, but as he began speaking, I was absolutely captivated. As he spoke, God fell on me in an unexpected way. I found myself praying, "God, if you let me live as long as that old man, I would like to be just like him." I got a transcript of that sermon that I keep in my file. By the way, the man's name was Vance Havner. I have many of his books and consider them to be treasures.

Today may have begun like any other day. You may not expect that anything special is headed your way. But somewhere out on the mountain God has called your name. Today He's got something for you. Who knows what God might do in just a moment? When He speaks, it is clear. When Elijah walks by and wraps his cloak around the young man, what he means is extremely clear. It means, "I as a prophet of God am spreading my influence and my leadership over your life. You now are under my authority, under my leadership. You now are with me." Clear. No questions. No doubt. Nobody speaks your name the way God does. And when God speaks to you, the call is extremely clear.

It also is concise. Elijah has no question about what God wants with him. He specifically is to go with Elijah, learn from him, and get ready for a life of ministry as a prophet himself. When asked, "Elisha, what does God want to do with your life?", he does not have to scratch his head and say, "Well, I don't know. I'm sure He's got something out there for me, but I don't know what it is." No! When he gets the call, it is concise. He knows what it is. Now we live in different days, but when God speaks and issues a call to us, it's still very concise. We have many options that sometimes can be confusing. I have talked with a lot of young people who say, "God has called me—I don't know what He has called me for, but He's called me for something." Now I want to tell you, if you'll get to the bottom of it, you'll find He has called you for something. He'll let you know exactly what that is. You can serve so many places in a church. Sometimes you might assume that a call from God means you either become a preacher or a missionary. But that is not the case. God has a plan and a purpose for every single one of His people. You never will discover a passion for God unless you have the sense of His call to some concise, specific ministry that He has tailor-made for you. Many in Christian vocations today are attempting to serve God without this burning passion derived from a concise call of God. The call of God is not to a vocation; it is to a life. It is not a career; it is a passion.

Please note that it can be canceled. Elisha says, "Let me kiss my father and mother good-by," and Elijah responds, in effect, "Do what you want to do. I don't have any hold over you." Elisha could have walked away from it. Over the years many have fought with God's call and purpose for their lives. They cancel the call. They say, "I'd rather do something else." Once you have heard God's call, you never will completely escape it. Always in the back of your mind will be a reminder of what might have been. Anyone who walks away from God's purpose for his or her life is destined to live out his or her life on less than God's best for that person. God has great plans for us all, but He will not force His purpose on you. You can say, "Lord, no", but you never will escape His call.

At the moment of God's call, it is consuming. Elisha is plowing with 12 yoke of oxen. Now this means a lot of things. It means he is from a wealthy family. If it were in our day, he might have been driving one of the fleet of vehicles that is in his family business. He's out operating one of the family bulldozers in the construction world. Yet, when he recognizes the call of God on his life, he takes the 12 pieces of plowing equipment and throws them in the fire to make a sacrifice to God, kills the oxen, and offers them as a sacrifice. He makes an absolute, final, and complete break with his former life. He now is consumed with God. I think of the words of Jesus Christ, who said, "No one who puts his hand to the plow and looks back is fit for service in the kingdom of God." When you acknowledge the call of God on your life, it is consuming. You will make a clean break with everything else. All that matters is the fulfillment of God's purpose. It puts the passion in your life. American Christianity has all the means we can ever need to take the good news of Jesus Christ to our world. What is missing is the consuming passion that has its source in the call of God. The moment of the call, it is clear, it is concise, it can be cancelled, and it is consuming.

THE MENTOR

Elisha needs a time of preparation. He is not mentioned again until 2 Kings 2, when Elijah is taken into heaven in a whirlwind. During that time he is with Elijah everywhere he goes. He is watching him walk, talk, speak, and pray. He is learning. He is an apprentice. The same thing happens with the Apostle Paul. He has an extended time of preparation. Barnabas mentors him. We all need a mentor. This mentorship occurs on the individual level. Elisha is there when one of the kings sends a group of 50 under a captain to go arrest Elijah. He hears them say, "Man of God, the King says, come down." He hears Elijah respond, "If I am a man of God, may fire come down from heaven and consume you and your 50 men." He sees the fire fall. He sees it happen a second time. Years later, Elijah is gone. A king has sent a contingent to arrest Elisha. His servant is panicking. Elijah assures him, "Those

who are with us are more than those who are with them."
"And Elisha prays, 'O Lord, open his eyes so that he may see.' The Lord opened the servant's eyes, and he looked and saw the hills full of horses and chariots of fire all around Elisha." He has learned well from his mentor; it blesses the kingdom of God. I have been blessed with some godly mentors in my life. We all need them.

In our churches today many warriors for Christ are mentors waiting to be asked. Our young people can learn much from these faithful laypersons who have served Christ and His church for decades. Many would be honored to bring a young layperson into their lives on a mentoring basis. This is the biblical model of growth! Find a mentor who's been there, done that, and will help you get there and do that, and will give you the basis to become someone else's mentor. Joshua had his Moses. Elisha had his Elijah. We all need a mentor. We all need an apprentice.

Not only did mentoring occur on the individual level, it occurred on the institutional level. A new institution appears. It is called, "The School of the Prophets." Elijah gets together some of these of like mind who have a heart for God; they band together. They strengthen each other and learn from each other. Elijah learns from his loneliness. He knows that we need others. We always can impact the kingdom in a greater way in a partnership than we can ever impact it alone. We need each other.

THE MINISTRY

Elisha's ministry is unique. Though Elisha performs more miracles, he never really attains the status of his mentor. Some apprentices do, but Elisha does not. God does not need another Elijah. God needs an Elisha. The same is true of Joshua and Moses. Look what Joshua does. He leads the people into the land, which Moses is unable to do. Even so, Joshua never quite attains the status of Moses. He does not need to. He does not need to fulfill Moses' life plan. He needs to fulfill his own. God is not looking for Moses the Second. He is looking for Joshua the First.

Avoid measuring your life by someone else's life. God does not need two of anybody. I have heard of many young guns given the mantle "the next Billy Graham." I'm not sure God is looking for the next Billy Graham. He needs the next YOU. Your ministry and your life are unique. The call of God can fall on your life in a thousand different ways. Everyone is different; the call is unique to each individual.

Not only is it unique, it also is unwavering. Difficult times occur in our lives when the call of God is all that keeps us going. That is what keeps Jeremiah in the ministry—the "fire in his bones." When Jesus asks Peter if he is leaving, as many others have, Peter says, "Lord, to whom shall we go? You have the words of eternal life" (John 6:68). This sense of God's hand and call on your life is what will keep the fire in your bones. In fact, that is the fire in our bones.

The call is unique, unwavering, and unbelievable. When you live in obedience to the call of God on your life, unbelievable things will happen to you. Elisha never would have seen the glory had he not been faithful to the call.

When you say "yes" to the call of God on your life, you open the door for God to do unbelievable things in your life. You will develop a passion that will drive you and excite you in all that you do.

THE MYSTERY

A mystery to God's call exists. People who live near the sea have the nature of the sea in them. They speak of the call of the sea. I play golf. I suppose I have the nature of a golfer in me. Every time I drive by a golf course, I can hear the call. Isaiah hears God's call as he worships. He has God's nature in him. He easily can hear and surrender to and embrace that call. The call may not be in an earthquake; it may not be in a ferocious wind or fire from heaven. It may be a still, small voice that is unmistakable. He knows your name. He is calling you.

Chapter 5

AN INCIDENT

1 Kings 21:1-22, 38; 2 Kings 9:24-10:17

The Scripture introduces this passage as "an incident." Indeed, it is quite an incident. Elijah is well into his ministry; his reputation is widespread. He is feared by those who do not love God; he is admired by those who do. His life and words are not ignored by anyone. Even in the throne room, the words of this preacher carry great weight.

Many years ago, on a Wednesday evening, a young preacher spoke to his congregation from this particular text. One of his men came to him afterward and said, "Now Pastor, I think you really got something there. You might want to work on that and hone it in, because there's really something in that passage and in that message." The young pastor, R.G. Lee, agreed and began to work on that message. He changed its title to "Payday Someday"; it became one of the most famous sermons in the history of Baptist life. Dr. R.G. Lee, pastor of the great Bellevue Baptist Church in Memphis, TN, preached that sermon thousands of times. God used it to impact thousands and thousands of people. Once one hears "Payday Some Day" as preached by Dr. Lee, one cannot possibly arrive at this passage of Scripture and not be influenced by that message. Nonetheless, this is quite an incident.

THE PLAYERS

You cannot know all the players in a ball game unless you have a program, just as you cannot fully understand this incident unless you know the players. We already have been introduced to Elijah. He is a man of God without equal. He is God's spokesperson, God's ambassador, and God's man for the hour.

Ahab is the king of Israel. He is one of the most powerful men on the planet. His nation is comprised of the northern section of the original Israel. A civil war has occurred after Solomon's kingship. This northern kingdom is named Israel; the southern kingdom is named Judah. The northern kingdom of Israel has abandoned the worship of Jehovah and worshiped the deities of the peoples who have previously lived in the land. Ahab has control of the armies of Israel, he has wonderful places to live, he has servants to serve him at his beckoned call, and he has won great military victories as the commander-in-chief of the armies of the northern kingdom. Though the master of his country, he cannot master his own lusts and his own greed. Sometimes talent and ability can take you to a place in which a flawed character cannot sustain you. Such is the case with Ahab.

Ahab's wife is the queen, Jezebel. She brought the worship of the gods of her country into this marriage and is probably the most wicked woman whose name is recorded in the Bible. No one today names his or her daughter Jezebel. She is the power behind the throne. She gives the king ideas and entices him to go places and do things he really did not want to do. The Bible describes these two in a footnote in which it says a man never existed like Ahab, who sold himself to do evil in the eyes of the Lord—urged on by Jezebel, his wife.

Another player in this incident is Naboth. Naboth is a citizen of the country. He is an honorable man, an honest man, and a forthright man. He is the kind of man that someone could build a city on, a country on, or a church on. He is the noblest kind of God-fearing man that Israel could produce.

THE PLOT

The Bible describes how these players are involved in the plot of this incident.

"Some time later there was an incident involving a vineyard belonging to Naboth the Jezreelite. The vineyard was in Jezreel, close to the palace of Ahab king of Samaria. Ahab said to Naboth, 'Let me have your vineyard to use for a vegetable garden, since it is close to my palace. In exchange I will give you a better vineyard or, if you prefer, I will pay you whatever it is worth.' But Naboth replied, 'The Lord forbid that I should give you the inheritance of my fathers.' So Ahab went home, sullen and angry, because Naboth the Jezreelite had said, 'I will not give you the inheritance of my fathers.' He lay on his bed sulking and refused to eat."

Nothing is inherently wrong in this request. Yet Naboth, an honorable man, realizes that God has given this property to his family as an inheritance from the time the Israelites arrive in the land of promise. The Mosaic Law teaches that property is to remain in the family's possession forever. Naboth desires to honor God, even if it means denying the king. The spoiled, arrogant, henpecked king pouts.

"His wife, Jezebel, came in and asked him, 'Why are you so sullen? Why won't you eat?' He answered her, 'Because I said to Naboth the Jezreelite,'Sell me your vineyard; or if you prefer, I will give you another vineyard in its place.' But he said, 'I will not give you my vineyard.' Jezebel his wife said, 'Is this how you act as king over Israel? Get up and eat! Cheer up. I'll get you the vineyard of Naboth the Jezreelite.' So she wrote letters in Ahab's name, placed his seal on them, and sent them to the elders and nobles who lived in Naboth's city with him. In those letters she wrote: 'Proclaim a day of fasting and seat Naboth in a prominent place among the people. But seat two scoundrels opposite him and have them testify that he has cursed both God and the king. Then take him out and stone him to death.' So the elders and nobles who lived in Naboth's city did as Jezebel had written to them. They proclaimed a fast and seated Naboth in a prominent place among the people. Then two scoundrels came and sat opposite him and brought charges against Naboth before the people, saying, 'Naboth has cursed both God and the king.' So they took him outside the city and stoned him to death. Then they sent word to Jezebel: 'Naboth has been stoned and is dead.' As soon as Jezebel heard that Naboth had been stoned to death, she said to Ahab, 'Get up and take possession of the vineyard of Naboth Jezreelite that he refused to sell you. He is no longer alive, but dead.' When Ahab heard that Naboth was dead, he got up and went down to take possession of Naboth's vineyard."

What an evil plot!—a good man surprised, betrayed, and killed. When the father and sons are killed, the land reverts to the crown. This is a quick, evil strike by an evil woman against an innocent man. The incident does not escape God's notice.

"Then the word of the Lord came to Elijah the Tishbite: 'Go down to meet Ahab king of Israel, who rules in Samaria. He is now in Naboth's vineyard, where he is gone to take possession of it. Say to him, 'This is what the Lord says: Have you not murdered a man and seized his property?' Then say to him, 'This is what the Lord says: In the place where dogs licked up Naboth's blood, dogs will lick up your blood—yes, yours!' Ahab said to Elijah, 'So you have found me, my enemy!' 'I have found you,' he answered, 'because you have sold yourself to do evil in the eyes of the Lord. I am going to bring disaster on you. I will consume your descendants and cut off from Ahab every last male in Israel—slave or free. I will make your house like that of Jeroboam son of Nebat and that of Baasha son of Ahijah, because you have provoked me to anger and have caused Israel to sin.' And also concerning Jezebel the Lord says: 'Dogs will devour Jezebel by the wall of Jezreel. Dogs will eat those belonging to Ahab who die in the city, and the birds of the air will feed on those who die in the country.'"

Ahab is enjoying himself in the vineyard when he hears the familiar voice of the preacher. In the desert God has spoken to Elijah. He exposes the secret plot and announces how God will respond. The wise among us today will consider how God will respond to our plans and plots.

The final part of the plot is the execution of judgment. About three years after Elijah's words, the judgment falls. Dr. Lee comments in "Payday Someday" that during those three years, every time Ahab hears a dog bark, he jumps. Ahab goes into battle, disguised so no one will recognize him as the king. Be mindful that when dealing with our Lord and Savior, even a seemingly random arrow is directed by His hand.

"But someone drew his bow at random and it hit the king of Israel between the sections of his armor. The king told his chariot driver, 'Wheel around and get me out of the fighting. I've been wounded.' All day long the battle raged, and the king was propped up in his chariot facing the Arameans. The blood from his wound ran onto the floor of the chariot, and that evening he died. As the sun was setting, a cry spread through the army: 'Every man to his town; everyone to his land.' So the king died and was brought to Samaria, and they buried him there. They washed the chariot at a pool in Samaria (where the prostitutes bathed), and the dogs licked up his blood, as the word of the Lord had declared."

Jezebel remains in the palace. Seventeen more years she lives and rules. Now Joram, the son, takes his father Ahab's place on the throne. Elijah already has gone to heaven. Elisha, the apprentice, now leads this prophetic ministry. God has given Elisha the word that the time for judgment on Jezebel has arrived. A man named Jehu is to execute the judgment.

"Then Jehu drew his bow and shot Joram between the shoulders. The arrow pierced his heart and he slumped down in his chariot. Jehu said to Bidkar, his chariot officer, 'Pick him up and throw him on the field that belonged to Naboth the Jezreelite. Remember how you and I were riding together in chariots behind Ahab his father when the Lord made this prophecy about him: 'Yesterday I saw the blood of Naboth and the blood of his sons', declares the Lord, 'and I will surely make you pay for it on this plot of ground', declares the Lord. 'Now then, pick him up and throw him on the plot, in accordance with the word of the Lord.'"

Jehu moves on down to Jezreel, where Jezebel is living.

"Then Jehu went to Jezreel. When Jezebel heard about it, she painted her eyes, arranged her hair and looked out of a window. As Jehu entered the gate, she asked, 'Have you come in peace, Zimri, you murderer of your master?' He looked up at the window and called out, 'Who is on my side? Who?' Two or three eunuchs looked down at him. 'Throw her down!' Jehu said. So they threw her down, and some of her blood splattered the wall and the horses as they trampled her underfoot. Jehu went in and ate and drank. 'Take care of that cursed woman,' he said, 'and bury her, for she was a king's daughter.' But when they went out to bury her, they found nothing except her skull, her feet and her hands. They went back and told Jehu, who said, 'This is the word of the Lord that he spoke through his servant Elijah the Tishbite: On the plot of ground at Jezreel dogs will devour Jezebel's flesh. Jezebel's body will be like refuse on the ground in the plot at Jezreel, so that no one will be able to say, "This is Jezebel."'

The parts the dogs do not want to eat are her skull containing the brain that hatched the plot, the hands that wrote the letter that caused Naboth to be killed, and the feet that walked on the vineyard.

THE PROPHETS

One great challenge from this incident is for our prophets. Our greatest need is not a booming economy or extensive prosperity. Our greatest need today is for a generation of God-called, God-anointed men who are not seeking to win a popularity contest but who are listening for a word from God to let their voices be heard. We need men with the fire of God in their bones. When God speaks to them in the desert, they are ready to preach that word in the palace. Ahab mistakenly refers to Elijah as his enemy. In reality, Elijah is his greatest friend, because he cares for his soul. Our pastors, preachers, and prophets must have a healthy fear of God with no fear of people. We do not love if we do not proclaim truth.

THE PRINCIPLES

We can learn much from this incident. Foremost is the principle of reaping and sowing (see Gal. 6:7-10). This principle is woven into our universe in both the natural and spiritual realms. That principle is universal in its scope and in its application.

We reap what we sow. Corn produces corn, wheat produces wheat, and peas produce peas, just as blessings produce blessings and evil produces evil. What Ahab and Jezebel sow in injustice and violence return to them in like kind. This is true on an individual scale as well as on a corporate scale. It is true for churches and for nations. It is true for all people—believers and non-believers. We all will reap what we sow.

We reap later than we sow. Twenty years is a long time. Jezebel surely thinks to herself that she has gotten away with it. Not so. God's judgment may be slow in arriving, but it grinds thoroughly and with justice. Nothing can be kept secret from God. Perhaps you think that no one knows how you slandered that person, lied on a business deal, or cheated on a spouse. Nobody knows! God knows. As Dr. Lee preached, "There is a payday someday." We are thankful for God's wonderful forgiveness in Jesus Christ but recognize consequences exist to our disobedience, even though we are forgiven.

We reap more than we sow. The harvest always is greater in volume than is the planting. We must be faithful to continue to sow to the Spirit while we realize that in due time, we will reap much more than we ever sowed.

THE PROLOGUE

Another aspect to address is the aspect from Naboth's viewpoint. Here a man of integrity, a man of joy, a man of obedience, and a man who loves God is brutalized, betrayed, and murdered. A wife becomes a widow, her sons murdered, and her possessions stolen. With all these injustices, why does not God step in and do something? Where is God during these times? Multitudes have asked the same questions. In the injustices of life, why doesn't God step in to help and deliver? Where is He when life is unfair, the finances fail, the home falls apart, or the doctor says, "malignant"?

I will tell you where He is. He's seated on the throne of the universe. His Son, Jesus Christ, has conquered death and hell. He's sent His Spirit to live within those who call on His name. I assure you with all the certainty of the truth of the Word of God that the day will arrive when every crooked line will be made straight and every injustice will be met with justice. So we say, "Lord, we trust You; we believe in You, even when the Ahabs and the Jezebels seem to have the upper hand. God wins! And we praise Him for it!"

So it's just an incident. Some Ahabs and some Jezebels may be reading this now. You have pulled off some stuff that is unbelievable; you have gotten away with it. No, you haven't. A payday will arrive. Some of you today are under the hand of a Jezebel or an Ahab. You have been mistreated, abused, and ostracized unjustly. God knows. He's going to get involved. He already is involved, although you may not yet be able to see His hand.

All of this—God's judgment and the unfairness of life—takes us to the cross of the Lord Jesus Christ. Apart from Jesus Christ we are all Ahabs and we are all Jezebels. However, in Jesus Christ we have cleansing, forgiveness, a new start, and redemption. We all can avoid a horrific payday by getting our lives lined up with God's purposes.

The ultimate payday—the ultimate incident—occurs at the cross and is confirmed by an empty tomb.

Chapter 6

PICK UP THE MANTLE

2 Kings 2:1-18

A crucial time always occurs for a country, a business or even a church when leadership changes. In any relay race, no matter how fast the runners are, the crucial moments are those times when the baton is passed. If the baton is not passed well, the race will not be won. If the baton is dropped during a change of leadership in a business, country, or church, problems and difficulties are certain. In the 2000 Presidential election, a problem occurred in passing the baton of leadership. Florida had difficulty counting the vote. For some time no one knew who was to become our next President. Various factions claimed the Presidency. In many countries, that would have resulted in a civil war or a revolution. Americans are grateful for the way our country changes leadership. Many churches experience adversity when leadership changes. The pastor who follows a long-term, beloved pastor usually has difficulty picking up the mantle of leadership. In the time of transition the leader must let go of the mantle of leadership for the new person to pick it up.

A time of transition has arrived for the ministry of Elijah. The time has arrived to pass the mantle of leadership to his God-chosen apprentice, Elisha. Elisha has prepared well.

Elijah's assignment from God has been completed. The cloak, or mantle, is the symbol of the prophetic office Elijah has occupied. The time is now for Elijah to let go of the mantle and for Elisha to pick it up.

Elijah's ministry has been one of power and fire. It has been a time of spiritual awakening, spiritual victory, and spiritual renewal. Both enemy and friend hold him in the highest regard. He has challenged and claimed victory over false gods, false prophets, and kings. Though he is an ordinary person beset by the challenges common to us all, by any definition his ministry is marked by success, power, and by the fire of God.

Elisha has witnessed it all. He knows the intimate details of Elijah's life much more deeply than do we who have our Bibles to inform us. He lives with Elijah, prays with him, supports him, and encourages him up close. He has seen him call down fire from heaven, challenge the king, and inspire his peers. For him to follow in this great man's footsteps will not be an easy task. However, every person's life will end until the return of our Lord Jesus Christ. Even the greatest among us will die. When they do, be assured that God has prepared someone to step into that person's place with "a double portion" of that person's spirit. In graphic language the Bible describes the changing of prophetic leadership.

"When the Lord was about to take Elijah up to heaven in a whirlwind, Elijah and Elisha were on their way from Gilgal. Elijah said to Elisha, 'Stay here; the Lord has sent me to Bethel.' But Elisha said, 'As surely as the Lord lives and as you live, I will not leave you.' So they went down to Bethel. The company (or the school) of the prophets at Bethel came out to Elisha and asked, 'Do you know that the Lord is going to take your master from you today?' 'Yes, I know,' Elisha replied, 'but do not speak of it.' Then Elijah said to him, 'Stay here, Elisha; the Lord has sent me to Jericho.' And he replied, 'As surely as the Lord lives and as you live, I will not leave you.' So they went to Jericho. The company of the prophets at Jericho went up to Elisha and asked him, 'Do you know that the Lord is going to take your master from you today?' 'Yes, I know,' he replied, 'but do not speak of it.' Then Elijah said to him, 'Stay here; the Lord has sent me to the Jordan.' And he replied, 'As surely as the Lord lives and as you live, I will not leave you.' So the two of them walked on. Fifty men of the company of the prophets went and stood at a distance, facing the place where Elijah and Elisha had stopped at the Jordan. Elijah took his cloak, rolled it up and struck the water with it. The water divided to the right and to the left, and the two of them crossed over on dry ground. When they had crossed, Elijah said to Elisha, 'Tell me, what can I do for you before I am taken from you?' 'Let me inherit a double portion of your spirit,' Elisha replied. 'You have asked a difficult thing,' Elijah said, 'yet if you see me when I am taken from you, it will be yours—otherwise not'" (2 Kings 2:1-10).

A TOUR

Elijah makes a farewell tour across the nation. His peers somehow know this is their final time to see him. They give great respect to the man of God. This peer group is called the company of the prophets. Other Bible translations call them the school of the prophets. This is a group of men called of God that Elijah assembles after he has been depressed and isolated in the desert. He thinks he is in the battle alone. God tells him he is not alone. In response to that revelation, Elijah gathers these men into a fraternity. They have been encouraging one another, supporting one another, and praying for one another. Together they are bringing the Word of God to Israel. They hold the man of God in the highest regard and give him the greatest respect.

In our culture, this regard and respect for the man of God is sorely missing. A handful of "pastor-friendly" churches hold in high regard the prophet of God sent to lead them, but the numbers of these churches are dwindling. Many reasons exist for this lack of respect. Sometimes this is because the pastor fails to live up to biblical standards for biblical leadership. Even if the person fails, God's people should hold the office of pastor in high regard. When they do, it motivates the man of God to live up to that respect.

Olen Miles was a great man of God. I was privileged to be his pastor for more than six years in Austin, Texas. On one occasion during a deacon's meeting he said, "I hold our pastor in high regard. I fear him, because God has His hand on his life." I never forgot that. I was unworthy to carry this great man's shoes. His respect for the office of the pastor motivated me never to do anything to disappoint him or others of his ilk in our congregation. Give your pastor honor and respect. Pray for him. Defend him. Support him. He needs that to stand up to the pressure of ministry demands in this day.

Even though Elijah's life is unparalleled in faith and power, people only can take us so far. As Elijah prepares his last will and testament, he asks Elisha how he can help in the transition. Elisha's response is, "I'd like to have a double portion of your spirit." Some believe Elisha is referring to the Mosaic Law that teaches that the firstborn child of the family gets a double portion over the other children. I believe that Elisha recognizes his life in comparison to the greatness of his mentor and believes that he needs God to bless with double power to make up for the deficiencies in his life. Yet he asks for something Elijah cannot give. Elijah cannot give someone

God's blessings and power. Only God can do that. When you die, you cannot leave to your heirs something you do not possess. Elijah can take Elisha only so far. The balance is in God's sovereignty.

In our day, people can plan, network, and advance in their field, but the anointing Elisha craves only can be sent from God. Much can be accomplished because of talent, creativity, and diligent work, but this anointing occurs only from above. Perhaps this is because our spiritual leaders have mastered their methods, honed their talent, planned their advancement, and worked the system to do God's work that we see little supernatural fire in our day. We are seeing God's work done in people's strength. We do not need more creativity, methods, or programs in our day. Where we are sorely lacking is in the realm of the anointing power of God on our lives. Oh, that we could call down the fire from heaven! Oh, that a generation of men of God with the same desire of Elisha would arise! Not only would the man of God be respected, but the Lord God would be honored among us.

Our pastors can bring us to the door of heaven, to the edge of the Jordan, but they cannot go in for us. They can take our hand and lead us to the place of decision, but they cannot decide for us. People can take us only so far.

A TRANSLATION

The next passage describes only the second experience of a man going to heaven without facing death. The other was Enoch.

"As they were walking along and talking together, suddenly a chariot of fire and horses of fire appeared and separated the two of them, and Elijah went up to heaven in a whirlwind.

Elisha saw this and cried out, 'My father! My father! The chariots and horsemen of Israel!' And Elisha saw him no more. Then he took hold of his own clothes and tore them apart" (2 Kings 2:11-12).

In our day, a great challenge arises to the claim of the Bible regarding the exclusive nature of salvation. If anyone holds the Bible in high regard and Jesus Christ as a man of integrity and truth, His words in John 14:6 cannot be disregarded:

"Jesus answered, 'I am the way and the truth and the life. No one comes to the Father except through me.'"

The claim that the way of Jesus Christ is the only valid way to eternal life only can be denied if the Scripture is denied or if Jesus Christ is teaching falsehood. What kind of heavenly Father would allow His Son to be crucified if another way existed?

Though only one Way exists to eternal life, we enter that way by many different paths. Elijah is taken to heaven suddenly. He is there one moment and is gone the next. He experiences an immediate translation into the presence of God. Years later Elisha gets to the same place, but he goes differently. The chariots arrive for Elisha, also, but do so a little differently.

"Now Elisha was suffering from the illness from which he died. Jehoash king of Israel went down to see him and wept over him. 'My father! My father!' he cried. 'The chariots and horsemen of Israel!'" (2 Kings 13:14).

The same chariots that picked up Elijah returned for Elisha. However, this did not happen so suddenly. Elisha suffered with illness. Those around him knew he was dying because of his illness. But, nonetheless, "the chariots and horsemen of Israel" arrived to take him into God's presence.

And so, different ways exist along the same path. The Bible says, "It is appointed unto man once to die, and after this comes the judgment." Some are translated quickly, perhaps from a heart attack or accident. Some linger for years as they suffer in an illness. Perhaps when those believers in Christ looked out of the windows of the airplanes about to crash into the Twin Towers on 9/11, what they saw looked more to them like the chariots of God and the horsemen of Israel swinging low to carry them home.

One of the greatest preachers of his time—Alexander Maclaren—lived in England. When he was a young man, he got his first job that was several miles from where he lived. He was scheduled to leave home for work Sunday afternoon, check in on Monday morning, and get off Friday afternoon. He had the weekend off. Between where he lived and where he was to work was a ravine that all the kids believed was haunted at night. He realized his trip home Friday evening would force him to cross the ravine after dark. After his father denied his request to wait until Saturday to come home, he realized he would have to face the haunted ravine. He thought about it all week. On Friday he hurried and hoped by chance he could cross the haunted ravine before the haunts came out. When he arrived, dark had fallen; he stopped at the edge of the ravine. With sweaty palms and a knot in his throat, he was about to turn and go back the way he came. A noise from the ravine caused him to freeze in fear. Then he heard the familiar voice of his father, "Alex, I've been longing to see you. I've come here to greet you and walk with you and bring you home." No one knows how the end of this life will arrive for him or her. One thing is certain—the chariots of God and the horsemen of Israel will be there to carry us home!

This translation of Elijah presents us a picture of the translation of the church at the return of the Lord Jesus Christ.

When our Lord returns, we will be caught up, without death, translated immediately, and escorted into the presence of Almighty God. The night is arriving when no one can work. Suddenly, as lightning flashing from east to west, in the twinkling of the eye, that trumpet will sound. The church will be changed. We are looking and longing for the chariots and horsemen of Israel!

A TRANSITION

The transition follows. The mantle of leadership falls. Elijah is gone. Somebody has to pick it up.

"He picked up the cloak that had fallen from Elijah and went back and stood on the bank of the Jordan. Then he took the cloak that had fallen from him and struck the water with it. 'Where now is the Lord, the God of Elijah?' he asked. When he struck the water, it divided to the right and to the left, and he crossed over. The company of the prophets from Jericho, who were watching, said, "The spirit of Elijah is resting on Elisha." And they went to meet him and bowed to the ground before him. 'Look,' they said, 'we your servants have fifty able men. Let them go and look for your master. Perhaps the Spirit of the Lord has picked him up and set him down on some mountain or in some valley.' 'No,' Elisha replied, 'do not send them.' But they persisted until he was too ashamed to refuse. So he said, 'Send them.' And they sent fifty men, who searched for three days but did not find him. When they returned to Elisha, who was staying in Jericho, he said to them, 'Didn't I tell you not to go?' (2 Kings 2:13-18).

A question is asked. Out of his loss and his pain and his sorrow and his need, an empty place exists in the heart of Elisha. His security and his mentor are gone. All he has left is this cloak—this mantle. It is a symbol of leadership; he says, "When Elijah was here, we heard from God. Elijah is now gone. I have the mantle, but where now is the power? Where is the God of Elijah?" Then an answer is given. With trembling hands, Elisha, holding that mantle, that cloak, eases on toward the edge of the Jordan River. On the other side are those 50 other preachers. He doesn't know if he has it in him or not. He lays that cloak to the edge of the water. And as soon as it touches the edge of the water, it begins to roll back. I am sure that no one is more amazed than Elisha. It is easy to do, because Elisha is not doing it; God was!

When God puts His hand on your life and you step out in obedience, you will be amazed at what God can do in your life. We ask the same question today. "Where is the God of Elijah, the God of Elisha?" He is at the same place He always has been. We see Jesus Christ on the cross dying and ask, "Where is the God of Elijah?" We see the tragedies that have occurred in our country in our time; we are devastated by the horror of it. We ask, "Where is the God of Elijah?" He is where He always has been and forever will be—seated on the throne of the universe. The earth is His footstool. He is sovereign; He has a plan.

The God of Elijah is within your reach right now. He is as near as your own heart. He is as near as your own mouth. With the heart we believe, with our mouth we confess, and by faith in the Lord Jesus Christ we enter God's kingdom. We know where the God of Elijah is. A greater question is, "Where are the Elijahs of God?" Some are in pulpits, to be sure. Most are ridiculed by a secular media, sometimes even by their own people. Some are still in the pews. The mantle has been laid at your feet. The time is now for you to pick up the mantle God has for you and move on with God's purpose for your life. Pick up the mantle!

Chapter 7

DITCH DIGGERS

2 Kings 3:11-25

Elijah and Elisha set the standard for prophets. They are certainly different kinds of men holding the same office. Elijah is a desert dweller—rough, direct. Fire is associated with his ministry. He is a man of extreme emotions—sometimes high, sometimes low—challenging 400 false prophets one day and running into the desert at the threat of Queen Jezebel on the next day. Elisha, on the other hand, is from a cultured family. He is comfortable in and out of the palace of kings. His ministry is composed of miracles that are gentle and that are blessed. Elisha's personality is a little quirky. If you were to talk to Elisha, he would appear to be mean and surly. Once you got past that outer layer, he would do whatever you asked him to do. The prophet's mantle passes from Elijah to Elisha; God is about to confirm this transition of the prophetic office.

He already has been confirmed before his contemporaries and peers when he divides the Jordan River with the mantle of Elijah. He then is affirmed as God's man in the ancient city of Jericho. The city where the walls have fallen has been rebuilt at the cost of the builder's firstborn son and youngest son. However, the water is bad. Elisha pours a bowl of salt into the water and makes it good. To the city of Jericho God says,

"This is my man." All follicle-challenged men can familiarize themselves with the last portion of 2 Kings 2. A group of young people are ridiculing Elisha, saying, "Go on up, you bald head." "Bald head" means someone who is losing his hair in the back. They are saying, "Go on up like Elijah did. Leave us alone." Since Elisha sometimes is mean and surly, he curses them in the name of the Lord. Cursing here does not refer to vile language but something like, "May God take care of you, boys." Two female bears emerge from the woods and tear apart 42 of them (we're not certain why the Bible identifies them as female bears; maybe those lads were in real trouble). The skeptics become aware that Elisha has the hand of God on him.

Elisha is confirmed before his peers, before the city of Jericho, and before the skeptics. Now he is to be confirmed before the king. A crisis is emerging for three aligned kings. Out of the crisis God speaks. In our crises he speaks most clearly. We have no doubt that American Christianity and America in general are in a state of crisis today. We need our Elishas to step up and speak a word for the Lord in times such as these. In the crisis of this text somebody seeks a word from the Lord.

"But Jehoshaphat asked, 'Is there no prophet of the Lord here, that we may inquire of the Lord through him?' An officer of the king of Israel answered, 'Elisha son of Shaphat is here. He used to pour water on the hands of Elijah.' Jehoshaphat said, 'The word of the Lord is with him.' So the king of Israel and Jehoshaphat and the king of Edom went down to him. Elisha said to the king of Israel, 'What do we have to do with each other? Go to the prophets of your father and the prophets of your mother.' 'No,' the king of Israel answered, 'because it was the Lord who called us three kings together to hand us over to Moab.' Elisha said, 'As surely as the Lord Almighty lives, whom I serve, if I did not have respect for the presence of Jehoshaphat king of Judah, I would not look at you or even notice you. But now bring me a harpist.' While the harpist was playing, the hand of the Lord came upon Elisha and he said, 'This is what the Lord says: Make this valley full of ditches. For this is what the Lord says: You will see neither wind nor rain, yet this valley will be filled with water, and you, your cattle and your other animals will drink.

"This is an easy thing in the eyes of the Lord; He will also hand Moab over to you. You will overthrow every fortified city and every major town. You will cut down every good tree, stop up all the springs, and ruin every good field with stones.' The next morning about the time for offering the sacrifice, there it was—water flowing from the direction of Edom! And the land was filled with water.

"Now all the Moabites had heard that the kings had come to fight against them; so every man, young and old, who could bear arms was called up and stationed on the border. When they got up early in the morning, the sun was shining on the water. To the Moabites across the way, the water looked red—like blood. 'That's blood!' they said. 'Those kings must have fought and slaughtered each other. Now to the plunder, Moab!' But when the Moabites came to the camp of Israel, the Israelites rose up and fought them until they fled. And the Israelites invaded the land and slaughtered the Moabites. They destroyed the towns, and each man threw a stone on every good field until it was covered. They stopped up all the springs and cut down every good tree. Only Kir Hareseth was left with its stones in place, but men armed with slings surrounded it and attacked it as well" (2 Kings 3:11-25).

In this crisis emerges the advice to dig ditches. God is seeking some ditch-diggers to answer the crises of our time.

Some questions that must be answered grow directly from this passage. The first question is;

WHERE DO YOU GO IN A CRISIS?

A challenge is before these three kings. Ahab, the wicked king of Israel has died, according to the prophecy of Elijah. Joram, his son, has taken Ahab's place. Though Joram is not as wicked as is his father, he is wicked, nonetheless. He is a worshiper of the false gods the people of the land worshiped before Joshua's conquest of the land. Moab, a country that has been in servitude to Ahab, has rebelled. Joram convinces the King of Judah—the good King Jehoshaphat—to join forces with him to put down the rebellion. Another king from the nation of Edom joins them. Their plans are about to turn to disaster, because the river where they are anticipating to yield water for their army is dry.

Three armies and no water around. Men and animals are in danger of dying.

The challenge has become a crisis. No one, except Jehoshaphat, knows what to do in the face of this dilemma. His counsel: "Let us seek the Lord." Where do you go in a crisis? No one's character is developed in a crisis. Character is revealed through adversity. This is how God reveals His champions. Without the crisis these kings might never have known Elisha. God uses adversity in our lives to reveal our character.

In times of adversity playing the blame game is easy. These kings could have blamed each other and made the crisis even worse. We may look at the challenges in our lives and find blaming the boss, or the employees, or the church, or just anybody other than the real culprit to be easier. Realize that the crises in our lives are designed to make us go deeper in our walk with God. They provide opportunities for our true character to shine. In this opportunity God can call out His champions to stand tall and true.

In 1999 I was diagnosed with cancer in my neck. Nothing will catch your attention like hearing the doctor from across his desk say to you, "It is malignant." I told the people of the great church which I pastor, "I have been preaching sermons to you; now I intend to live one before you." I can happily share that God took care of that chapter of adversity in my life; I have experienced His presence and power to a degree I never could have without the adversity.

Notice they do not begin to seek God until they have no relief in sight. All their plans and all their resources are gone. They have no way to get water; they have no ideas or plans. They have exhausted all their resources. The last thing they can do is call on the Lord. Much progress in human development has been made since this time, but we still are the same way. In the face of adversity, we put together all our resources, all our abilities, and all our networks. We pull all our switches; we do all we can think of. When nothing works, we finally say, "I've done all I know to do. It's up to God now! I have no recourse but to trust Him." The truth is, from the beginning God has been trying to get us to this place.

Where do you go in a crisis? The best place to go is to the presence of the Lord.

DOES THE HEART OF THE GODLY HAVE RESPECT FOR YOUR PRESENCE?

What a question! To paraphrase Elisha's response to these kings, "What do we have to do with each other? Go to the prophets of your father and the prophets of your mother. That is who you worship. Why come to me? If I did not have respect for the presence of Jehoshaphat king of Judah, I would not look at or even notice you." Obviously, Elisha hasn't been to the counseling school of our day. I guess you would call that compassionate conservatism.

When a crisis arrives in life, some might call the commissioner of the National Football League and ask him what they need to do, because that is who they worship. Some might call their broker, because they worship their money. I am convinced that some men who are alive today have not been judged by Almighty God because they have wives whom God respects. Their prayers are holding back God's hand of judgment. I believe the opposite is true, as well. Some women with a sharp, poison tongue have avoided the judgment of God because He holds their husbands in respect. Some fathers and mothers have little children praying to God for their parents; those prayers are holding back the judgment of God on them. God has held together some businesses because He has respect for their employees.

Do the hearts of the godly have respect for your presence? Only you can answer that. Joram knows it is not there for him. He knows he had no relationship with God. Jehoshaphat has that respect. It is because he loves the Lord and nurtures his relationship with Him.

HOW DO YOU HEAR FROM GOD?

This may be one of the greatest questions of our day. How do you hear from God? Note that Elisha calls for a harpist. He probably is burning on the inside—righteously indignant, angry. Hearing God when you are angry is difficult. As a young preacher, the advice that to preach when angry will be "the greatest sermon I would ever regret" rings true. Music is a window into our soul. As they play, Elisha calms down and allows himself to get balanced and into a position to hear God.

In church buildings all over our world, people arrive for worship who are hurting—who need a word from God. The praise through music calms hearts, heals souls, and prepares the spirit to hear from God. When King Saul is tormented, he has David play the harp because it soothes him. Music really is a window into our soul. The harpist plays; Elisha intentionally seeks to hear from God. God speaks and Elisha hears a word from God.

When any of us intentionally and intently seeks to hear a word from God, it is available. A soothed spirit and an open Bible create an environment for us to hear the Spirit of the Lord Jesus Christ speak to us. Avoid bowing before God asking for a blessing on a decision already made, but have a heart to receive whatever He brings to us.

Elisha's answer is nothing short of incredible. This is an easy thing in the eyes of the Lord. What is about to put these three kings under is an easy thing to the Lord. No matter what challenge we face, to God it is an easy thing. When God speaks, peace rolls over our spirits; we realize that in the presence of our God all our crises are easy matters for Him. I heard of a woman who told her pastor that she did not bother God with the small things—only the big ones. The pastor's reply was on target: "Ma'am, to God all our things are small." The reason some never hear from God is that they never get into a position to hear from Him. We're too busy being mad, too busy complaining, too busy trying to correct the problems ourselves, too busy to just sit and listen and get soothed in our hearts to hear Him. It's always an easy thing.

WILL YOU OBEY?

The final question is huge. Elisha gives them the information they ask for. The word from the Lord is, "Dig ditches. Fill the valley with ditches." That does not make a lot of sense. These armies are on the verge of battle and about to die of thirst; God says to dig ditches. They will not see storms, but God is going to fill the ditches with water. Not only that, but God is about to give them more than they ask for—a complete victory. That is just like the Lord. He gives over and above what we can ask or think. "Not only will you get water so you'll live, but I'm going to give you a great victory over these Moabites." They do what God asks of them. They fill the valley with ditches. God honors and blesses their obedience. Up in the mountains of Edom behind them, evidently and probably, arrives a great rain storm that they do not even see in the valley. The rain water fills those ditches! They awake in the morning and have not received a bit of rain, yet the ditches have filled overnight. Everything God gives is wonderful. I'm convinced that water was cold and good.

The Moabites across the way get up that morning, too. They look over at those opposing armies. All they see is red. The hills of Moab are made of red clay. The combinations of the morning sun and the reflection off the water look as though a bloodbath has occurred in the camp. Not expecting a fight, they enter the camp and are surprised by a well-prepared army. The rout is on.

You may face a great challenge in your life. Most of us usually are just getting out of some adversity, are in the midst of it, or soon will enter into a season of adversity. You may be thirsty to hear from God. But to do that, you need to dig you a ditch. Fill your heart with ditches. When God speaks, will you obey?

Dig you a ditch; prepare for God to bless you. From all we experience in our world today, we know that the days are evil. We believe that time is short. I recently learned that two of my contemporaries in the pastoral ministry have died. Work while you have day, for night comes when no man can work. Before you know it, those little children will be leaving your home. One day you will wake up and be a senior adult. Someone said, "We are dying men preaching to dying men." Life is too short for you to wait any longer before you dig you a ditch.

Dig you a ditch in your family life. Get with your wife or your husband and your kids and fly a clear banner in your home: "We are a Christian family. We're living for God here."

Dig you a ditch in your private life where nobody else has access. In that private life dig you a ditch and say, "My heart, my life belongs to Jesus Christ."

Dig you a ditch in your public life. Whether your career or your school is involved, dig you a ditch and stand without shame for Jesus Christ. The crisis of 9/11 made standing for Jesus Christ easier than ever. God did this out of a crisis. From that crisis we were blessed to see the Christian soul of our nation stand up; all the little peripheral groups that have been nipping at everybody's heart for years scurried back under the rocks. They did not stay there long. What kind of crisis will it take for God's people to dig a ditch that will stand the test of time in our public lives?

Dig a ditch in your church life. The only hope for America and for our world is the message that the Body of Christ presents to this world—the saving message of Jesus Christ. You need to dig a ditch, find your place in the Body of Christ, and become a part of God's solution.

Where do you go in a crisis? Run to Jesus Christ. Dig a ditch. Does the heart of the godly have respect for your presence? Make it so by your lifestyle. Dig a ditch.

How do you hear from God? You hear Him through the Word of God speaking in that still, small voice to your heart. Dig a ditch.

Will you obey Him today? Dig a ditch.

Chapter 8

BRING ME ANOTHER JAR

2 Kings 4:1-7

Elisha has been confirmed as God's man. His ministry begins now that he has been established as the successor to Elijah. His peers, his skeptics, and his kings have acknowledged him as a man of God. Plausibly Jehoshaphat, the King of Judah who fears the Lord, can bring Elisha to Jerusalem to be close to him. That does not happen. However, God does not send Elisha to minister only to those in king's palaces but to any and all of God's people. As Jesus Christ later will model, Elisha's ministry turns to the common people in out-of-the-way places living ordinary lives. How wonderful that the glory of Jesus Christ is not confined to princes and presidents but is available to paupers like me. Elisha begins to perform private miracles unnoticed by others yet resounding in heaven. Through this miracle God has a word for us. That word is, "Bring me another jar."

"The wife of a man from the company of the prophets cried out to Elisha, 'Your servant my husband is dead, and you know he revered the Lord. But now his creditor is coming to take my two boys as his slaves.' Elisha replied to her, 'How can I help you? Tell me, what do you have in your house?' 'Your servant has nothing there at all,' she said, 'except a little oil.' Elisha said, 'Go around and ask all your neighbors for empty jars. Don't ask for just a few. Then go inside and shut the door behind you and your sons. Pour oil into all the jars, and as each is filled, put it to one side.' She left him and afterward shut the door behind her and her sons. They brought the jars to her and she kept pouring. When all the jars were full, she said to her son, 'Bring me another one.' But he replied, 'There is not a jar left.' Then the oil stopped flowing. She went and told the man of God, and he said, 'Go, sell the oil and pay your debts. You and your sons can live on what is left' (2 Kings 4:1-7).

TIMES THAT ARE HARD

One can read through that passage and almost skip over the situation that the prophet's widow faces. You can just read it and not even think about her. However, she is in quite a bind. She is a woman with two children whose husband is a prophet of God and has never had much, according to worldly standards. In fact, while he is living, her husband had outstanding debts. His unexpected death leaves his widow with two small sons. According to the Law of Moses when people have debts they cannot pay, their children are subject to be taken as slaves until the debt can be paid. In the year of Jubilee, every 50th year, they will be freed. This lady's difficult times include not only the death of her husband but the prospect of losing her sons as well.

In my preaching I sometimes take "side streets." This passage requires a brief "side street." In every Christian denomination are many great servants of God who have lived their entire lives in obedience to God's call and purposes for their lives. They have served as pastors or staff members of churches all over our country. They are easy to overlook. Many of them now have retired or left widows who are living on extremely meager incomes. In my denomination alone, the Southern Baptist Convention, are more than 8,000 retirees or widows receiving less than $200 per month on which to live from their retirement plan. Their average age is 77; their total average monthly income is about $860, while their average monthly expense is a little over $1,000. If at all possible, we need to be Elishas to these dear people. The church I serve is involved in our denomination's Adopt an Annuitant program. Let's take care of those servants of God as best we can.

Now back to the prophet's widow. She is in a rough spot. When rough spots like this arrive, oftentimes the people wonder. They wonder why bad things happen to good people. Recorded in Jeremiah 12:1-2 is this question of the great prophet:

"You are always righteous, O Lord, when I bring a case before you. Yet I would speak to you about your justice: Why does the way of the wicked prosper? Why do all the faithless live at ease?"

Jeremiah has a question about God's justice. The faithful servants of God seemed to suffer horrible tragedies, while those who have no pretension to love God have all the blessings. At one time or another we've all asked that common question. We believe that those who love God should be delivered from tragedy, while those who do not should have some additional adversity in their lives.

I am not wise enough to have all the answers, but I do know that growing from those difficult times are the finest opportunities for us to grow into the depth and width of the love of Jesus Christ and to give evidence of the reality of our faith. This miracle would not have occurred had the widow not had these difficult times. The encouragement over the centuries that has been afforded millions from this miracle would have been absent had the widow not suffered the difficult times. The same is true for us all. Your children would not see your faith in action had those difficult times not arisen. You would never have experienced God's deliverance had not the difficult times occurred. Remember that out of these crises of life, a cure always arises. We all experience times that are difficult.

TRUST FROM THE HEART

Notice the favor Elisha extends the woman. She explains her predicament; Elisha gives her a plan of action. To her credit, she has enough trust in Elisha to do what he says.

Time for another "side street." Many shysters and hucksters are in the pulpits of America today and on television. They want your money. I would not trust some of them with a single nickel. Many people have reason to distrust those speaking for God. Deep in my heart I long for the day when God's people begin to trust God's prophets again. For God to visit us again in spiritual awakening and renewal, we must regain integrity in the pulpits in our land. For every shyster that is exposed are probably thousands of men of integrity whose ministries suffer and become more difficult because of them.

This widow listens to the prophet, trusts God, and does what is asked of her. I am not the greatest counselor in the world. I see few shades of gray. An issue or an action is right or wrong. I cannot possibly count how many times a person has asked me what I think he or she should do in a particular situation. In response to a biblical answer I give, that person will say, "I don't think I want to do that." What they want to hear is a stamp of approval for what they already had done. This widow listens to Elisha and does what he asks of her. In doing so, she says, "I'm going to trust God; I'm going to obey."

The two preacher's kids now invade the neighborhood. They go to their neighbors and ask for empty jars. The widow is pouring from a flask—a little pouch or sack—containing a small amount of anointing oil that you would put on your body. The boys keep bringing the jars; she just keeps pouring. She fills up one jar, then another jar and another. The miracle occurs as she is pouring. "Bring me another jar," she says. They say, "We don't have any more." They all stop. Notice the shortcoming: she could have had more. The only limits on this miracle are the limits she imposes herself. If more jars had been available, more oil would have been available. In one sense, the widow shortchanges herself. Elisha's advice again is followed as she can sell enough oil to pay the creditors, keep her boys, and live off the rest.

That is a wonderful thing for this widow. What about the flow to our lives? I'm convinced that all people desire oil to flow into and through their lives like that. Three great truths must occur for that to happen: 1. Give God what you have; 2. Bring Him an empty jar; 3. Keep bringing empty jars.

Give God what you have. When the widow asks what Elisha can do for her, his response is, "What do you have in your house?" That is God's question for you. What do you have in your house? Give what you have in your house to God. You will be amazed at what God can do with just a little bit that is really given over to Him. God could have done this miracle without this little flask of oil. But in her giving Him what is in her house, she makes the statement, "Not only am I giving to God what I have, I am giving to God who I am." He is getting ready to start the flow into her life so she can become a fellow worker with Him.

If you would like to see the flow into your life, give God what you have. Doubtless, we have a whole lot more than this woman has. She has one little jar of oil. To give God what you have at your house, simply tell Him it is His. I give You my automobile. I give You my furniture. I give You my bank accounts. I give You my clothing. I give You the relationships in my home. I give You my business, my career. Give everything in your house to the Lord Jesus Christ. You will discover that you will become a fellow worker with Jesus Christ as well. You will be getting into a position for the oil to begin flowing in your life. It will result in glory to Jesus Christ and blessings to you.

Bring an empty jar. Possibly while this widow is pouring the oil, she turns to pour into one jar, but no oil emerges. Maybe they look in that jar and it still has something in it. They have to eliminate that jar because it is not empty. We must give to God an empty jar.

No one will go very far with God by turning over a new leaf. That is because the new leaf that you turn over in a few days will be another old dead leaf. Jesus Christ does not desire to take the old stuff and make it a little bit better. The key that unlocks the door of victorious Christian living is in this idea of bringing to Christ an empty jar. This little phrase succinctly expresses it:

"Not I, but Christ."

That phrase is from Galatians 2:20:

"I have been crucified with Christ and I no longer live, but Christ lives in me. The life I live in the body, I live by faith in the Son of God, who loved me and gave Himself for me."

That is bringing Jesus Christ an empty jar. None of us has anything Christ needs. In fact, sometimes our best traits can become our worst deficiencies, because we trust our abilities rather than trusting the Lord Jesus Christ. He does not want what we have; He wants us. To bring Him an empty jar means that you give Him the title deed to your life with no strings attached. That is a radical commitment. That is what is required to see the oil flow.

If you really desire to see God flow incredible things into your life, tell Him, "Lord, here is my life. No strings are attached whatsoever." Not very many people will make that kind of commitment. Not many people see the oil flow. Many will tell the Lord that as long He leaves a part of their life alone, as long as He leaves the pocketbook alone, as long as He leaves the recreation plans alone, as long as He leaves the private moments alone, He can have everything else. Yet if you really have a thirst for God to pour Himself into your life, make your commitment with no conditions.

During my seminary days I met a great friend. As we shared our dreams and hopes for how God might use us, my friend shared that he was willing to do anything and go anywhere God desired as long as it was in a certain area of our country. He was committed with conditions. His was not an empty jar. He did serve two congregations in that part of our country. Both wore him out and wore him down. He no longer is in the ministry. If we fill our jar, we will exhaust the contents. If God fills it, the contents will be new every morning.

My wife and I began our pastoral ministry in a small, farming community in Oklahoma. Our income was below the poverty level. Our commitment to give beyond the tithe never wavered. We still have some of those budget sheets. Our outflow always was more than our income. I have no idea how it all worked out, but I know that it did work out. No bill was left unpaid. God kept pouring the oil into the empty jars.

Keep bringing Him empty jars. You can stop the flow. God keeps giving Himself as long as we bring to Him that into which He can pour Himself. When we stop bringing, He stops pouring. Fast-forward for a moment to another passage that expresses this same idea. Elisha is about to die; the king of Israel arrives to visit him one last time. This is found in 2 Kings 13:15-19.

"Elisha said, 'Get a bow and some arrows,' and he did so. 'Take the bow in your hands,' he said to the king of Israel. When he had taken it, Elisha put his hands on the king's hands. 'Open the east window,' he said, and he opened it. 'Shoot!' Elisha said, and he shot. 'The Lord's arrow of victory, the arrow of victory over Aram!' Elisha declared. 'You will completely destroy the Arameans at Aphek.' Then he said, 'Take the arrows,' and the king took them. Elisha told him, 'Strike the ground.' He struck it three times and stopped. The man of God was angry with him and said, 'You should have struck the ground five or six times; then you would have defeated Aram and completely destroyed it. But now you will defeat it only three times.'"

Now I don't understand all of that, but what I do understand is that this king of Israel limits what God is going to do because he hits the ground only three times and stops. The widow limits what God would have given her because she brings a limited number of jars. Continue to bring Him empty jars. The provision of God is not exhausted—only the number of jars. More supply is available if she only would bring more jars. They would still be pouring oil today if they had kept the jars arriving. When I read this passage, I always think, "Dear woman, why didn't you bring more jars? I know that is all you could find, but why didn't you go find some more? Why did you stop? God had a lot more for you.'"

Some have not had a fresh movement of the Spirit of God in their lives or church in a long, long time. Maybe you have not brought Him an empty jar in a long, long time. The reasons that they did not get any more jars were many. These two boys may have gotten lazy or bored bringing the jars. They may have gotten sidetracked. Something else may have captured their interest. They just did not bring any more. Some may have gotten spiritually lazy. Some perhaps are sidetracked. Some may become satisfied with less than God's best. Some say the blessings of the past are enough; we have enough to live on. That is why the crises in our lives can destroy us. We are living on some old oil from an old jar delivered a long time ago. God's provision and blessings never run dry. We just run out of jars.

The day you stopped serving Him is the day the oil stopped. The day you quit using your spiritual gift in ministry is the day the oil stopped. The day you began to embrace known sin and rebellion in your life is the day the oil stopped. The day you stopped bringing Him an empty jar is the day the oil stopped.

God's provision and blessings never run dry. We just run out of jars. His word to us today is, "Bring me another jar!"

Chapter 9

SEVEN SNEEZES

2 Kings 4:32-37

Miracles sometimes occur in the lives of unknown people. Such is the case in 2 Kings 4:32-37. This miracle doesn't contain a lot of glitter and glitz as do a couple of the other previous miracles in Elisha's life. I'll set the stage and then move in for some closer detail. Here is a wealthy woman who has spent some time with Elisha and recognizes him as a man of God.

She and her husband decide they want to do something for him. Their gift is a room built onto their house where he could stay when he was in the area. The King James Version calls it the "prophet's chamber." I have preached in revival meetings and been the guest in the homes of church members who had built on a prophet's chamber. Many do not appreciate Elisha's ministry, so encountering someone who desires to make his life better likely is a breath of fresh air.

God gives her a son. Sometime later the son dies. Possibly he has a heat stroke. This unnamed woman goes to the prophet and says, "I didn't ask for this child. God gave him to me. Now I'm going through this heartache." Elisha sends his servant, Gehazi, ahead where the child is, in the prophet's chamber, with instructions to lay Elisha's staff on the head of the child. He does that with no results. The dead child does not respond. Elisha arrives . . . .

"When Elisha reached the house, there was the boy lying dead on his couch. He went in, shut the door on the two of them and prayed to the Lord. Then he got on the bed and lay upon the boy, mouth to mouth, eyes to eyes, hands to hands. As he stretched himself out upon him, the boy's body grew warm. Elisha turned away and walked back and forth in the room and then got on the bed and stretched out upon him once more. The boy sneezed seven times and then opened his eyes. Elisha summoned Gehazi and said, 'Call the Shunammite.' And he did. When she came, he said, 'Take your son.' She came in, fell at his feet and bowed to the ground. Then she took her son and went out" (2 Kings 4:32-37).

From this miracle we can discern some incredible life principles. They are true for all of us, no matter our status in life. Join me as we discover them.

GOD BLESSES YOU WHEN YOU ARE A BLESSING

Notice the woman's gift. It is really a little thing in the overall picture of life, but to this man of God, it is an awesome thing. He had kings who would like to have him killed. To a lot of people he was very unpopular. How refreshing for this man who was serving at the command and in obedience to God to find somebody who will actually bless him with no strings attached! It is an awesome thing.

A couple in our church in Austin, Texas, owned a beach house in Gulf Shores, Alabama. The couple decided that any pastor or staff member of the church could go down there anytime it was available at no cost whatsoever. What an awesome thing for someone to say, "Here is a gift with no strings attached!" The Pritchard family has been to the couple's home at least nine times. The memories with our family and the refreshment from those times cannot be measured. As I write this, I am at the vacation home of some beloved friends and church members who have made their house available to me for this purpose. I cannot tell you all God has done in their lives, but I promise you, they have been and will be blessed. Other passages of Scripture confirm this principle.

"Anyone who receives a prophet because he is a prophet will receive a prophet's reward, and anyone who receives a righteous man because he is a righteous man will receive a righteous man's reward. And if anyone gives even a cup of cold water to one of these little ones because he is my disciple, I tell you the truth, he will certainly not lose his reward" (Matt. 10:41-42).

Check out the Apostle Paul's take on this principle:

"I have received full payment and even more; I am amply supplied, now that I have received from Epaphroditus the gifts you sent. They are a fragrant offering, an acceptable sacrifice, pleasing to God. And my God will meet all your needs according to his glorious riches in Christ Jesus" (Phil. 4:18-19).

The principle proves true as we consider the woman's blessing. To the Hebrew mindset, the inability to have children is considered a curse. Though they are wealthy, this husband and wife are considered cursed because they have no children. In return for their being a blessing, God returns a great blessing to them. This must not be twisted into a "give-in-order-to-get" scam. The woman gives out of the love in her heart and expects nothing in return. She believes in him, loves him, and loves the Lord. She simply wants to be a blessing to Elisha.

Be a blesser, and you will be blessed!

HARDSHIPS OCCUR WITH EVERYONE

This promised child dies. Nothing is more difficult for anyone to deal with than to have a child die. No one looks forward to losing anyone to death. Yet, in the natural order of things, we recognize that our parents probably will die before we do. As married couples age, either the husband or wife will die, then the other. For a parent to lose a child is not in the natural order of things. This is a good woman. But remember, hardships occur with all of us. In this hardship and in every hardship a divine purpose exists in it all. Several years later an amazing thing happens in this very same woman's life.

"Now Elisha had said to the woman whose son he had restored to life, 'Go away with your family and stay for a while wherever you can, because the Lord has decreed a famine in the land that will last seven years.' The woman proceeded to do as the man of God said. She and her family went away and stayed in the land of the Philistines seven years. At the end of the seven years she came back from the land of the Philistines and went to the king to beg for her house and land. The king was talking to Gehazi, the servant of the man of God, and had said, 'Tell me about all the great things Elisha has done.' Just as Gehazi was telling the king how Elisha had restored the dead to life, the woman whose son Elisha had brought back to life came to beg the king for her house and land.

"Gehazi said, 'This is the woman, my lord the king, and this is her son whom Elisha restored to life.' The king asked the woman about it, and she told him. Then he assigned an official to her case and said to him, 'Give back everything that belonged to her, including all the income from her land from the day she left the country until now'" (2 Kings 8:1-6).

This is an incredible display of the sovereignty of God!

The fact that just as the woman approaches the King, he is talking about her is no accident! The open theists have a lot of circumstances to explain. Our lives have no accidents in them—only a divine purpose in everything, including the hardships. When hardships arrive and you cannot understand God's purpose, you can trust Him implicitly to hold your life in His hand.

Hardships become the grounds for prayer. This woman really has an awesome moment in prayer when she lay before Elisha. After Elisha sends the servant ahead, she refuses to let go of him. Gehazi is a fine servant, but she needs more than he can deliver. She is saying to Elisha, "You made the prophecy, I am clinging to you for the answer." That is a tremendous ground for prayer. God has made us untold promises in the Word of God. By giving us these promises, He extends us the privilege of claiming them as our own. Sometimes the hardships and challenges we do not understand cause us to stretch out before Him and cling to Him until we do understand. Hardships take us to our most hallowed praying ground.

KEEP PLANTING SEEDS

Elisha's first strategy does not work. The lad does not respond to Gehazi's laying the staff on him. Elisha changes strategy to the next plan and goes himself. We need to understand that God's work has partnership in it. Paul wrote, "What, after all, is Apollos? And what is Paul? Only servants, through whom you came to believe—as the Lord has assigned to each his task. I planted the seed, Apollos watered it, but God made it grow. So neither he who plants nor he who waters is anything, but only God, who makes things grow. The man who plants and the man who waters have one purpose, and each will be rewarded according to his own labor. For we are God's fellow workers; you are God's field, God's building" (1 Cor. 3:5-9).

A partnership exists in God's work. You plant a seed at one place, someone else adds a word, and it all ends up being a blessing to the Lord.

"Sow your seed in the morning, and at evening let not your hands be idle, for you do not know which will succeed, whether this or that, or whether both will do equally well" (Eccl. 11:6).

Gehazi, do your thing. Now Elisha, do yours. Who knows which will bring the project to fruition? The bottom line is that God gets the glory. Sow seeds in the morning, sow seeds in the evening, sow seeds. And so keep planting these seeds. None is more difficult to reach than someone like this child who is dead—if he was reachable! If you are up against a difficult person or a hardship, keep planting seeds, because you never know when God will break through.

As you keep planting seeds, avoid the Gehazi spirit. I am not certain, but I think that Gehazi's attempt at a miracle is the only time in the Old Testament a miracle is attempted that does not happen. Gehazi is to put the staff on the child, which he did, and nothing happened.

Elisha is staying at Mt. Carmel, the site where the fire of God has fallen in the days of Elijah. How interesting that he wants to live close to where the fire fell! It is about a three- to four-hour trip to the woman's home. Though Elisha does not really want to make the trip, at the woman's persistence he does. Darkness likely has fallen when they meet Gehazi with the news that nothing has happened. Where is the problem? Is it with the boy, with the mother, with the staff, with Gehazi, or with Elisha? An amazing thing—a prophet's staff not doing a prophet's work. The problem cannot be with the child; the child is dead. It cannot be with the mother; she has made her request. It cannot be with Elisha, because everything he touches, God blesses. And it cannot be with the staff, because it returns unbroken. The problem must be Gehazi.

Let's think about Gehazi. Perhaps a prophet's staff only has its power when it is wielded by the hand of a prophet. A few years after this event a man named Naaman, who has leprosy, approaches Elisha with leprosy and is cured. He offers gifts to Elisha, but Elisha refuses. After Naaman leaves, Gehazi secretly chases him down and receives some of his gifts. Gehazi's true character is revealed. He has a problem with greed, lying, and other things. So when he wields the staff of the prophet, it has no power. A prophet's staff only has its power when the hand of a prophet wields it.

We have in our hands the Word of God. Often much power doesn't seem to be released. Personally, many Sundays nothing has happened after I have taken the staff of God and placed it on my people and proclaimed the Word of God! I have retreated to the study and said, "O God, is something wrong with me?" Realize that we have the eternal Word of God on the pages of this Book. We are to wield it and to teach it and to live it and to share it. When you put the tools of a prophet in the hands of the prophet, God will move in power. When we wield the word of God and nothing happens—the child doesn't awake—don't blame the staff, the Bible, or the Lord.

We need God to help us look into our own hearts. A prophet's staff has its power only when the hand of a prophet wields it. Perhaps you are like Gehazi, holding forth a prophet's staff, but in reality, you know it's not in the prophet's hand. Your life is so dry spiritually that no one is being blessed through you. Maybe the time to clean up your life has arrived. Perhaps God's Word to you is not "take your son" but "take your life, take your life back. Get in step with Me. Get where you need to be." Avoid the Gehazi spirit.

As you keep planting seeds, be mindful that no other person can do your work. This work called for Elisha; Gehazi could not do it. Every one of us who truly knows Christ has a purpose and a place within the church. No one else can fill that purpose and that place. Nobody else can do your work. God has provided you a staff. Pick it up and fill your position in the Body of Christ. If you refuse, somebody somewhere is missing a blessing only you can bring. No other person can do your work.

GOD GIVES LIFE

This final principle from this miracle is awesome. The words in that last verse to the woman are, "Take your son." I would have liked to have been there to see what happened. It is after dark in the prophet's chamber. It is a very familiar place to him, and yet on the couch the boy lies dead. The room surely is dimly lit; the mother is weeping. She hears footsteps in the chamber. She hears a sneeze. Then another—seven in all. Mothers recognize their children's sneezes. Could this be the boy? Gehazi arrives at the door and says, "Ma'am, Elisha's calling for you in the prophet's chamber." As she opens the door, she sees the boy—alive and very well! What words: "take your son." What a moment!

God gives life! Out of tragedy, out of hardship, out of misunderstandings, God's purpose and design always are to give you life. He is not trying to mess up your plans. He is not trying to cramp your lifestyle. He wants to give you life. As we read how Elisha lies on the boy and prays, walks back and forth, and lies on the boy and prays, I think about how easily

Jesus Christ raises Lazarus from the dead. Remember? All he had to do is say, "Lazarus! Come forth!" And the dead man, who has been dead four days, emerges from out of his grave. I believe that had not Jesus Christ qualified that command—had He just said, "Come forth!", everyone who had ever died would have come forth. But He says, "Lazarus, you're the only one I'm calling now." The day will arrive when He will call the name of everyone who knows Him. He will complete the gift of eternal life He gave us at the moment of our salvation.

Perhaps as you read, you realize you are somewhat like this boy. You were spiritually alive, but now you are empty and dry. Someone laid a staff on you, but nothing happened. Listen for the voice of Jesus Christ calling your name. The message He has for you is life—eternal and abundant.

God always gives life.

Chapter 10

WILD VINES

2 Kings 4:38-41

The miracle of the wild vine involves some everyday events of life and does not really lend itself to the glitz and the glamour of what one would expect from a miracle. However, some tremendous truths spring from this miracle of Elisha. Plenty of wild vines are in our world today. If anyone puts fruit from these wild vines in his or her life, it will bring difficulty, pain, and even death to that person.

"Elisha returned to Gilgal, and there was a famine in that region. While the company of prophets is meeting with him, he said to his servant, 'Put on the large pot and cook some stew for these men.' One of them went out into the fields to gather herbs and found a wild vine. He gathered some of its gourds and filled the fold of his cloak. When he returned, he cut them up into the pot of stew, though no one knew what they were. The stew was poured out for the men, but as they began to eat it, they cried out, 'O man of God, there is death in the pot!' And they could not eat it. Elisha said, 'Get some flour.' He put it into the pot and said, "Serve it to the people to eat.' And there was nothing harmful in the pot" (2 Kings 4:38-41).

We intentionally bring some harmful things into our lives. Sometimes unintentionally we give harmful things access to our lives. Computer viruses can gain access to one's computer and destroy much work in a very short time and can render the computer virtually useless. The fruit of harmful things—intentional and unintentional—can do the same things to us. In just a few short moments they can destroy a lifetime of good work. They can render someone virtually useless in that person's work for the Lord Jesus Christ. We can learn much from this miracle of wild vines.

"WILD-VINE" VALUES WILL BRING DEATH TO YOUR POT

Self-centered values are wild-vine values. They will bring death and destruction into your pot and into your life and into your family. Self-centered values are values that one's own judgment determines. This value system is known as moral relativism. For a couple of generations existentialism philosophy has been the guiding concept for the educational system in our universities. This philosophy teaches that right and wrong is determined by the individual on the basis of what is right for him or her according to the circumstances of the moment and the feelings that are dominant at the time of the decision. The new term for existentialism is moral relativism. For those who are living by self-centered values, right and wrong is determined by how they feel at any given moment. No objective truth from which to make decisions exists. It is all relative.

What parents taught regarding right and wrong no longer are the deciding factors for those living with these values. To these, the Bible was true for the people of the first century but not for those in our day. No grounds exist for morality, because no absolutes exist. If something is right for you, no matter what the Scriptures teach, it is right. Wrong and right then are determined by how one perceives what is best for him or her at a given time.

Marriages and families are being torn apart in alarming fashion because decisions are made through the grid of moral relativism. The argument goes something like this: My husband/wife no longer is making me happy. I know that God wants me to be happy. Therefore, divorcing him/her is right and good and moral. This is the right thing for me to do because it is right by my judgment and values at this time in my life. God approves, because this is what I believe.

These self-centered values that our people are bringing into their lives are bringing death to the pot. This moral relativism also has brought us to our present climate of political correctness. Our society has become so open-minded that our brains have fallen out!

Another offshoot of this death in the pot is pluralism. Since no absolute truth exists, everyone's idea of truth is equally valid with any truth claim. Everybody is right all the time; no one is wrong. No one has the right to suggest that someone else is wrong. No one has the right to claim truth on his or her side. Everybody is right and moral all the time in every situation. According to pluralism, every religious system is equal in value and truth. The claim of Jesus Christ that He is the Way, the Truth, and the Life, and that no one comes to the Father except through Him flies directly in the face of pluralism. Jesus Christ teaches that one narrow Way; that is His way. The current conviction that different paths will take one to the same place defies even the most basic logic. Different descriptions of God, different ways of salvation, different values of life, and different bases for truth cannot take you to the same place. Since moral relativism teaches that no objective right or wrong exists, then all people are right, no matter what they believe. Using the logic of moral relativism, pluralism, and political correctness, one could not condemn the atrocities of Adolf Hitler. He, along with the German authorities, believed they were right. The Allies believed they were wrong. If no objective basis to determine right and wrong exists, how dare the Allies suggest they were right and Hitler was wrong! After all, aren't all belief systems equally valid? If Nazi Germany had arrived on the scene in this day, we might not have had the moral fortitude to fight it.

Pluralism and political correctness have brought death to the pot. They are wild vines.

If self-centered values are wild-vine values and bring death to your pot, then Savior-centered values bring healing to your pot. Where does one find these values that bring healing and life? They are in our Bible. It is the Word of God. What God says about integrity, about honesty, about morality, about sin, about forgiveness, about faith, hope, and love, about heaven, about hell, about humankind, and about Himself is true for all people at all times. When you adopt a position that says, "I'm not the one who determines the values of my life; the Word of God does", you are putting healing in your pot—in your life.

One evening when I was on a statewide, radio call-in show, a gentleman called and was somewhat upset. After a couple of comments, he cut to the chase, "Well, Preacher, how do you know what God thinks about anything?" My response was quick and sure, "God has told us what He thinks about every issue facing us in our lives. He told us in His Word, the Bible." Our values and value judgments that should hold us as followers of Christ are clearly laid out in the Bible for us to read and embrace. I have discovered that when one is captivated by the Lord Jesus Christ, he does not grip these convictions; they grip him!

Many people have their lives falling apart around them. They have conformed to the culture in which we live and have based their decisions on moral relativism rather than on Christ-centered values. They have gone against the ancient wisdom of God, have written their own code of conduct, and are paying a high price. Death is in the pot. Many among us are glad to receive the Bible truths about forgiveness and heaven but remain committed to self-centered values regarding everyday life. If anyone has acknowledged Jesus Christ as Savior and Lord, that person must adopt His value system for life. With no exceptions God honors and blesses obedience to His Word every time. It puts healing into our lives.

Let's consider the marriage issue and the Nazi Germany issue in regard to the Word of God. God never would change His eternal Word or His mind regarding marriage because someone is in a period of time in which he or she does not feel happy. To believe that God would change His mind and go against the teachings of the eternal Word of God because one person is having difficulty with a spouse at a certain moment is bizarre. Only someone whose life revolves around himself or herself could ever entertain such a notion. For the disciple of Jesus Christ, life is not about that person; it is about Jesus Christ. God's standard is one man and one woman in a committed relationship for life. That is what He desires.

Hitler was wrong because his value system was not Savior-centered but was self-centered. The atrocities of his regime were morally upright to him and his cohorts, but in the final analysis they were immoral because they violated the values of the Bible. The Allies recognized the values of our Western civilization and acted in defense of those values. The values on which our entire civilization as well as our country are based have their roots firmly planted in the Mosaic Law—the first five books of the Old Testament in our Bible.

Self-centered values, moral relativism, and political correctness are wild vines. They will bring death to the pot. Savior-centered values—honoring and obeying the Word of God—will bring healing to the pot. Our culture has been described as the Culture of Death, much in part to the champions of abortion and euthanasia, the twin fruits of relativism and pluralism. This has happened because of the wild vines whose fruit has been thrown into the pot. Only a return to the Lord Jesus Christ and His teachings will give us the healing we need to become a Culture of Life.

"WILD-VINE" RELATIONSHIPS WILL BRING DEATH TO YOUR POT

Unbalanced relationships are wild-vine relationships. They will bring death into your pot. Balanced relationships bring healing to your pot. The most crucial aspect of our lives is our relationships. If a person's relationships are unhealthy and unbalanced, no matter what else is good in his or her life, that life is unhealthy and usually unhappy. Addictions, behaviors, and attitudes that are destructive all are derivatives from relationships out of balance. If a person's relationships are good, healthy, and balanced, the opposite is true. No matter what else is present or absent from the life, the life is good, blessed, and joyful. Unbalanced relationships bring destruction. Balanced relationships bring life.

Three basic areas of relationship exist in our lives. The first is our relationship with the Master. Only Jesus Christ can balance your life in that deep, inner place. The basic biblical truth that we all have sinned is true for every one of us. Our spiritual life is out of balance. We suffer with guilt, shame, and depression because we do things we do not desire. Often we intentionally bring things into our lives that we know will destroy us. We struggle with our sin nature. To regain your balance spiritually, have a moment in time in which you begin a true relationship with Jesus Christ. Acknowledge that He died on the Cross for your sin payment, that He was raised from the dead, and that He lives today. The reality of that relationship becomes the cornerstone for every other relationship in your life.

That relationship deepens with time and growth. Learn how to die to self and live to Him. Learn the blessings and joy of obedience as well as the pain of disobedience. The Christian life is a journey of growth, excitement, and joy in the midst of it all. The greatest relationship on your way to a balanced life is the relationship with the Master.

The second area of relationship to balance is your relationship with other people. These relationships begin at home and spread to all those around us. Many men struggle with life because of a relationship with their dad that was without depth, affection, or involvement. A hole is in their hearts. The same is true for many women. Parental neglect has caused them to be unbalanced with their husbands and children. No greater human relationships exist than those in the family. In the context of family young men learn how to become fathers and husbands. There they learn what it means to be men. In the context of family young women learn what being wives and mothers means. There they learn what being women really means. Today young men go out into the world to become husbands and dads and have no idea what that even means. Young women become wives and mothers and have no model before them of what that means. No wonder we have gender confusion in our day. Men have lost the biblical grasp of manhood as women have lost the biblical ideals of womanhood. If mom and dad are confused, the children have no option but to continue in and often deepen that confusion. Based on the relationship with the Master, ground your relationships in the home on biblical truth.

A huge aspect of this balance with others is the biblical principle of being equally yoked. This concept teaches that the intimate relationships in our lives have their basis in a common faith in the Lord Jesus Christ. Young people: understand that a marriage to a nonbeliever is putting a wild vine in the pot. Though exceptions exist, untold numbers of young men and women marry someone who did not share their faith; their lives have become tragic and painful. They put death in the pot. Parents: teach this concept to your children beginning when they are at an early age.

Not only make a common faith in Christ the basis for marriage, make it the basis for intimate friendships. I have heard literally hundreds of testimonies of people throughout the years. A testimony is someone's "God story." Almost every person whose story includes a life of destruction before he or she knows Jesus Christ begins with this phrase or one like it: "I began running around with the wrong crowd." Becoming intimate friends with people who do not follow Jesus Christ is a wild vine. It brings death to the pot: they will not be raised up by their relationship with you but rather will drag you down into their lifestyle.

Also, maintain balanced relationships with friends, co-workers, relatives, and acquaintances. Conflict and disagreements can make our lives so out of balance that bitterness takes over our lives. This is the fruit of a wild vine. Each of us has had experiences with other people that hurt us, often very deeply. We have all been slandered, misunderstood, taken advantage of, and mistreated in many other ways. At this point make a critical decision. Based on how Jesus Christ has forgiven you, forgive those who have wronged you. Forgiveness is not a feeling. It is a choice. If you choose to forgive, soon enough the feelings of forgiveness will catch up. The healing process will begin; the pain of the mistreatment will fade. I know many people living lives characterized by bitterness. They are chronic complainers and seem to find the bad and negative in every situation. Someone has said that these kinds of people live longer. Someone then corrected the statement to say, "They don't actually live longer; to everyone else they just seem to!" Somewhere in their lives they were hurt deeply and did not forgive. The resulting bitterness has colored the way they live and view life. It put death in the pot. If you choose to forgive, bitterness will not rule your life.

Across my many years as a pastor serving our Lord, I have experienced many painful moments. One particular incident was extremely hurtful. In this incident my wife and I made a decision to be loving and forgiving to all involved. Today I can honestly say that I have no resentment or bitterness in my heart toward any of the people involved. In fact, I can hardly remember the details of the incident, because my feelings have caught up to my decision to forgive. It put healing in the pot.

I'll make one other note regarding our relationship with others. None of us can go through life without offending others. Most of the time, hopefully, it is unintentional. To put healing in your life and in the lives of others, take the initiative to seek forgiveness from those you have hurt. Get alone with God. He will remind you of those who are hurting because of your attitude, word, or deed that offended them. Go to that person and seek reconciliation by seeking their forgiveness without rationalizing your behavior. It not only will bring healing to you, it will bring healing to them.

A third great relationship that must be balanced is the relationship with "me." So many are suffering from such a low self-esteem that they cannot possibly balance any other relationship in their lives. How else can the cosmetic surgery craze be explained? People do not like the way they are, so they go to great lengths to improve. Those who are in Christ recognize that He loves us just the way we are. We present ourselves to Him as we are and find that he does not reject or ridicule us. He loves us as we are. In fact, He loves us too much to leave us the way He finds us. As He brings balance to our inner lives, we begin to realize that we are of great worth to God. We are able to maintain a healthy, balanced relationship with ourselves.

In Jesus Christ, we can like who we are. We can enjoy our thoughts and our places in God's plan. We do not have to measure ourselves against others, but we have the freedom to be who God created us to be. That is balance. That is healing in the pot.

Without balance with the Master and balance with others, balance with "me' is impossible. Unbalanced relationships bring death to the pot. Destructive lifestyle, addictions, and attitudes spring from unbalanced relationships. Balanced relationships bring healing. Balance with the Master, with others, and with myself brings life, health, and joy into your life. Get balanced. It will bring healing to you.

"WILD-VINE" LIFESTYLES WILL BRING DEATH TO YOUR POT

A self-centered lifestyle is a wild-vine lifestyle. Your values determine your lifestyle. If your values are self-centered, your lifestyle will be unacceptable. It will bring the fruit of a wild vine into your life. Whether at work, recreation, or relaxation, relationships will not make any difference, because all that matters is you. The lifestyle is all about you. It is a lifestyle that grows from the attitude of "me first" and results in using people and hurting others in order to satisfy personal desires and ambitions.

The result is a lonely life empty of meaningful relationships. Usually a marriage or two gets destroyed along the way. Children are left longing for a close relationship to mom or dad but find this impossible because mom and dad are all about themselves. Their values are self-centered, as their lives become. Career advancement as well as financial gain occurs, but at the center of life is emptiness. Going from one fad to the next, attempt after attempt is made to fulfill that inner place, but more fruit from more wild vines is thrown into the pot. The lifestyle becomes one of death and destruction. Children experience this kind of lifestyle and emulate it. The culture of death is passed from generation to generation. Death is in the pot.

Few things are as painful and hurtful to the Kingdom of God than people who say, "I love Jesus Christ, I love the Bible, and I love the church," but their lifestyle, their presence, and their finances say something altogether different. Something is not right with that. Death is in that pot. Preachers who preach, singers who sing, deacons who serve, members who attend—if the lifestyle does not match the confession of their faith, hypocrisy reigns in the church, the Spirit of God is quenched, and our ministries are reduced to religious activities that keep people busy. Yet few lives are changed; certainly, the culture is not engaged. Rather than life, power, peace, and joy in the religious pot, death is in the pot, because the lifestyle does not match the confession of faith.

An acceptable lifestyle will bring healing to your pot. Nothing is finer or more beautiful than to know and be around people who say they believe in Jesus Christ and love the Bible and love the church and to see that their lifestyle backs that up. That is healing and is encouraging and is awesome.

Regaining integrity of lifestyle is imperative for God's people. Time has arrived for us not only to say we adopt and adhere to the values of the Bible but that we live them before a wandering generation. Trust that God will honor that. Trust that through a life of integrity your witness will be empowered by the Holy Spirit to impact lives and to affect eternity. As God's person be the healing of life that is thrown into the pot of this culture of death.

A "WILD-VINE" ANTIDOTE WILL BRING HEALING TO YOUR POT

Elisha takes the flour and throws it in the pot. It probably becomes some of the finest stew that ever touches the lips of humankind. The antidote for our culture of death is threefold. The first is the Lordship of Jesus Christ. When Jesus Christ is the Lord of our lives, by definition He also is the Lord of our relationships and the Lord of our lifestyle. He is our Authority, He is the One we seek to please, love, and honor. In our families, careers, and church life, He is in first place and brings healing and balance into our lives.

The second antidote is our knowledge of the Bible. Don't allow the moral relativists and the gurus of political correctness to determine your values or agendas. Through your study of the Word of God read and learn God's mind and heart.

His purposes are not revealed in your feelings but in His Word.

You only will discover the mind and heart of Jesus Christ as you spend time in the pages of His book. That puts healing in the pot.

A third antidote is involvement in the local church. In the local church accountability issues are addressed. Friendships there will hold you up and hold you accountable. They will be concerned for you and miss you when you are not there. The church is the only institution I know that is designed to make your family stronger and not designed to tear it down. Virtually everything else in our world is designed to tear our families apart. In your local church you'll find someone to help you, to stand with you in crises, and to help you through the tough times in life that we all have. Involvement in the local church will put healing in your pot.

Moral relativism, political correctness, and pluralism are wild vines whose fruit has put death in the pot. Ours is a culture of death. Ambassadors of Jesus Christ are the flour that can change that culture of death into one of life. We can do it through an acknowledgement of Jesus Christ as Lord, an ever-increasing knowledge and adherence to biblical truth, and involvement in our local church. Let's get to it!

Chapter 11

TAKE A DIP

2 Kings 5

Perhaps the most familiar of all the events in the life of the prophet Elisha is the healing of a man named Naaman. All of us can take a dip, as Naaman ultimately does, as we desire God to do a great work in our lives. The chapter tells of a young woman who has lost her home and her sense of community when a raiding party conquers her town and takes her into captivity as a slave. She works in the home of a man named Naaman, a general and a commander of an army of the king of Aram, from Syria. Naaman is good to this slave girl. Even though she has been taken from her home, she has grown to respect Naaman and to be concerned for him. Naaman is afflicted with a disease called leprosy. This was one of the most dreaded diseases of biblical times. It is a skin disease that eats away at the flesh. After a while, it slowly eats away the extremities in a very painful and slow process. In Israel, the Law of Moses requires those afflicted with leprosy to yell "unclean, unclean!" when they approach anyone. That lets those they approach realize they are about to encounter someone with this disease.

    Though probably not in its end stage, Naaman's leprosy is a horrible disease. The slave girl boasts to the wife of Naaman that if he lived in Samaria, a prophet who lives there could cure him. On sharing this with Naaman, the king grants him permission to go to Samaria and see this great prophet. When you become desperate, you will do many things to find relief. The key to spiritual awakening in our time is not that we desire it, but that we get desperate for it. Become desperate enough to do things out of the ordinary to see God move! Someone has well said that the best definition of insanity is doing the same things in the same ways and expecting different results. Desperate to be healed Naaman steps out of his comfort zone and heads to Samaria.

On arriving in Samaria, he goes to the king. He probably thinks that the King of Israel will be well-acquainted with a prophet so famous and powerful. However, the king finds himself powerless. In fact, he believes that Naaman is picking a fight with him by asking him to deliver something that is beyond his ability. When Elisha hears about the king of Israel's response, he sends him one of the most powerful messages recorded in our Bible:

"Have the man come to me and he will know that there is a prophet in Israel" (2 Kings 5:8b).

When Naaman arrives at Elisha's door, the prophet does not bother to greet him. He simply sends word for him to take a dip—in fact, to take seven dips in the Jordan River. He then will be cleansed and healed of his leprosy. Naaman grows upset because Elisha is so aloof. Naaman believes he is more important than that. That preacher does not even venture outside to see him! Besides, the rivers where he lives are cleaner than was the river Jordan. His advisors encourage him to do what Elisha says. In doing so Naaman is healed of his leprosy. The Bible says that his skin is restored like that of a young boy.

His attitude changes toward Elisha and, more importantly, toward Elisha's God. He attempts to pay Elisha with a gift that would have made the prophet wealthy, but Elisha refuses. Naaman does take some dirt back with him to symbolically worship the God of Elisha. He becomes a believer when he experiences the power. As he leaves, Elisha's servant, Gehazi, who has witnessed the entire event, gives in to greed, chases down Naaman, receives from him some of the gift previously offered to Elisha, and returns. This does not escape Elisha's notice. As a judgment for his greed, the leprosy of Naaman falls on Gehazi and his descendants forever. A keynote text in this section of Scripture is:

When Elisha the man of God heard that the king of Israel had torn his robes, he sent him this message: "Why have you torn your robes? Have the man come to me and he will know that there is a prophet in Israel" (2 Kings 5:8).

In our New Testament Jesus Christ also mentions Naaman.

"I tell you the truth," he continued, "no prophet is accepted in his hometown. I assure you that there were many widows in Israel in Elijah's time, when the sky was shut for three and a half years and there was a severe famine throughout the land. Yet Elijah was not sent to any of them, but to a widow in Zarephath in the region of Sidon. And there were many in Israel with leprosy in the time of Elisha the prophet, yet not one of them was cleansed—only Naaman the Syrian" (Luke 4:24-27).

The people of his hometown of Nazareth are so infuriated by His statement that they prepare to kill Him. The Jewish leaders of Jesus' day believe that as God's chosen people, they are the only ones that matter. They believe that if someone desires to know God, they can become a Jew and get in on the blessing. That is sort of the mentality of some churches. "If someone wants to get right with God, they know where the church is." That is directly opposed to our Lord's mandate to take the good news to the highways and byways as we live our lives. However, the Lord's statement raises a huge question. So many in Elisha's time have leprosy, yet only this Syrian is healed. Why doesn't Elisha heal them all?

Why doesn't God heal everybody in our day? Why isn't the "name-it-and-claim-it" gospel true? Why don't those with the supposed "gift of healing" empty a few hospital cancer wards? Why can't you just call out what you want and God be obligated to do it? One very simple reason exists. If that were true, then you would be God. If you could just name what you want and say, "That's mine", then God becomes nothing more than a messenger boy at your whim. That theology is degrading to Almighty God and not true to Scripture. Even the Apostle Paul struggles with a physical challenge:

"To keep me from becoming conceited because of these surpassingly great revelations, there was given me a thorn in my flesh, a messenger of Satan, to torment me. Three times I pleaded with the Lord to take it away from me. But he said to me, 'My grace is sufficient for you, for my power is made perfect in weakness.' Therefore I will boast all the more gladly about my weaknesses, so that Christ's power may rest on me. That is why, for Christ's sake, I delight in weaknesses, in insults, in hardships, in persecutions, in difficulties. For when I am weak, then I am strong" (2 Cor. 12:7-10).

The Apostle Paul is unable to call on God to heal on demand. Neither can we. Yet God is in the miracle-giving business. I believe in miracles.

Take your focus off the miraculous and put it on the One who can perform the miracles. Strive to get into a position in which God can touch your life with a miracle. We can get into that position as we consider the character qualities of the people in this incredible story.

THE HERO

The hero in this chapter is the unnamed slave girl. If anyone has a reason to be upset, bitter, and mad at God and everybody else, it is she. Taken from her home, family, and country, she now lives with people she does not know—a culture unfamiliar to her—where gods she knows are false are worshiped. Her life has been turned upside down. She understandably could have been bitter, happy that her master has leprosy, and certainly never be willing to offer assistance to him. But that's not the case with her.

She maintains a confident faith in God. Although hardship has arrived in her life, she has supreme confidence in God's prophet. Scripture never mentions her again. Naaman's response to her when he returns is anybody's guess. This unnamed servant girl has long since passed from this life without further fanfare or distinction. Yet she is a hero. She is one who honored God above all else. She is the one who believed God. I often wonder if this miracle was the way God honored her faith more so than He did the ministry of Elisha. In every miracle, somebody has to believe God. That somebody may be someone in the shadows such as this servant girl.

Untold numbers of heroes in our churches faithfully serve Jesus Christ in good times and in difficult times. They are faithful witnesses. They are faithful at their work; they are faithful with their lives. They are faithful with their finances. They are saying a good word about the Lord Jesus Christ, a good word about their church, a good word about their pastor and their staff. They may never get in the limelight and never get recognized as they should, but they are modern-day heroes. They believe God. They are the basic building blocks for the kingdom of God. That is what many of you are; you are heroes.

Recently a fellow pastor told me, "Some of your people have talked to me. They were highly complimentary of your staff." I thought, "I am glad to hear that we have some heroes out there that are talking well about the Lord, about the church, and about the staff." They have the spirit of this servant girl and in good times and bad they consider stepping up and giving a good word for Jesus Christ, His church, and His prophets to be a privilege. May the numbers of the heroes increase!

THE HIGH AND MIGHTY

In this miracle story the king of Israel is the high and mighty. As a king he is designed to be God's representative. When this opportunity arises for God to show Himself to be a Mighty God, he does not have a clue. The fact that another mighty man, Elisha, is in his kingdom never even crosses his mind. He is too busy building his own kingdom and protecting his legacy. He does not have time for all this; he is the high and mighty king. Note his name does not appear in the chapter.

Many people are building their own little kingdoms. They are aware of all the intricacies of goal-setting, networking, and becoming successful. Yet when someone speaks to them about spiritual things, they have no clue.

"Brothers, think of what you were when you were called. Not many of you were wise by human standards; not many were influential; not many were of noble birth. But God chose the foolish things of the world to shame the wise; God chose the weak things of the world to shame the strong" (1 Cor. 1:26-27).

That's sort of like choosing a servant girl as a hero over a high and mighty king.

In my freshman year of college I read a parable that has stuck with me through the years. A young ant had begun his adult life and found himself at the bottom of an ant hill. Others like him began to climb, so he began to climb, as well. As he fought his way up the ant hill, he sometimes had to climb over a fellow ant that had lost his grip and had to navigate past older ants that were on their way down. He never really understood why he was climbing, just that he had to climb. After a tremendous amount of work, he finally reached the pinnacle. As he pulled himself to the top of the ant hill, he paused for the first time in his climb to take in the view. He was astonished to find that no one noticed his feat and that other ant hills were as far as he could see across the horizon, with ants trying to get to the top as frantically as he had been trying to get to the top of his. It startled him so that he lost his footing for just a moment then another ant pulled him down. He was caught in the downward spiral like the older ants he had encountered earlier.

Many high and mighty are among us climbing their own ant hill—building their own kingdom for reasons they do not even know. In the process, they often lose their families, rupture many relationships, and tragically, miss God. They do not have a clue about spiritual things.

THE HYPOCRITE

No story could be complete without one. Gehazi, servant to the great prophet, fits the bill. He is so close. He is perhaps in line to become the successor to Elisha as Elisha has been to Elijah. He has seen miracles, experienced the power of God even to raise the dead, and other absolutely astonishing things. He is so close, yet he is so far. The lure and glitter of the treasure that will turn to dust in his hands causes him to give up his place.

"Gehazi, the servant of Elisha, the man of God, said to himself, 'My master was too easy on Naaman, this Aramean, by not accepting from him what he brought. As surely as the Lord lives, I will run after him and get something from him'" (2 Kings 5:20).

I don't know what happened. Perhaps while Naaman is talking to Elisha after the miracle and Elisha has declined the gifts, he catches a look in Gehazi's eye or sees some body language. However, Elisha knows Gehazi has sold out to the world. He runs after Naaman and receives a couple of little pieces of silver and a couple of sets of clothes, which was considerable treasure then. When Elisha confronts him, Gehazi denies he has done anything. He proves to be both a liar and a thief. What a horrible moment it must have been when Elisha says,

"'Was not my spirit with you when the man got down from his chariot to meet you? Is this the time to take money, or to accept clothes, olive groves, vineyards, flocks, herds, or menservants or maidservants? Naaman's leprosy will cling to you and your descendants forever.' Then Gehazi went from Elisha's presence and he was leprous, as white as snow" (2 Kings 5:26-27).

He sells his soul for two pieces of silver and two sets of clothes. Gehazi appears to be one thing, but he is something else. His ability and talent has taken him to a place in which his character cannot sustain him.

He has a lot of counterparts in the church of today. They are so close. God is doing miraculous, awesome, glorious, unexplainable things in our day. Many live so close yet remain so far away because their souls have been sold to treasures that eventually will crumble and turn to dust in their hands.

Gehazi sells out for a pittance; many sell out today for even less. Gehazi's sin not only affects him, it affects his descendants.

I suppose the church always will have hypocrites in it. Perhaps you are living in a family with a legacy like Gehazi's. Someone in your family has adopted a stance that has affected you; now it is filtering to your children. What a powerful thing if you take a stand for Christ and declare that halfhearted commitment to Christ will end right here with you! Pass something else down to your family worth passing rather than passing on the legacy of leprosy.

Many have said they will have nothing to do with the church because of the hypocrites who worship and try to pass themselves off as something they are not. Would not it have been totally ridiculous for Naaman to say, "Well, you know, that Gehazi is a hypocrite. I am not going to see Elisha because a hypocrite is in the house." The fact that Gehazi is a hypocrite has nothing to do with Naaman getting his miracle. And for you and me, the fact that hypocrites probably are in the house should have nothing to do with how we are dealing with our Lord Jesus Christ. Let the hypocrites hang around; let the Lord take care of them. Do not allow anyone to stop you from having a miracle touch on your life that you really need.

THE HALO

Elisha is wearing the halo this time. Notice his confidence. He is ready for the leper to visit him. He has confidence that Naaman will recognize that a prophet of God is in Israel. Some might see that as arrogance rather than confidence. Those who believe this have a misplaced understanding.

When a person is walking with Jesus Christ in the quiet place, dead to self and alive to Him, that person will brim with confidence. That confidence is not in himself or herself but in the Lord Jesus Christ. Elisha is totally confident in God's ability to shine through.

Notice he is kind of cool. Naaman pulls in with his great entourage and chariots and soldiers. Rather than going out to meet this important man, Elisha sends him a message. Elisha is tuned in to Almighty God. He really does not care about all those things. He has already seen the horsemen and chariots of heaven. He cannot be impressed, because he has been in the presence of God. Nothing can impress you more than that.

So he's cool and confident. When you get into the presence of the Lord in the quiet place, sometimes you may appear to others to be a little bit overconfident. You realize the confidence is not in yourself but in the power of the Lord Jesus Christ. We must with confidence in the Lord Jesus and with coolness toward the glitz of our world take our stand for our God. Our world still needs to know that prophets are in our world.

THE HEALED

Naaman is a proud man. He is a good man and treats his servants well. The soldiers around him pull for him, so he has good relationships. Yet he is so full of pride, he is offended that the preacher does not emerge and make a fuss over him.

He also has some preconceptions. He thinks he knows a better way to conduct this miracle than does the man of God! Preconceptions can cause you to miss God's blessing on your life. God is not locked in to work in ways that fit our preconceived ideas and programs. Break out of the spiritual ruts in your life; give the Spirit freedom to do His work in the way He chooses.

Naaman also is penitent. He finally does what Elisha asks. He dips not once, or twice, but seven times. Partial obedience would not have resulted in his healing. Six would not do; only seven would suffice. When he dips that seventh time, he is changed, not only outwardly, but inwardly. He gets that miracle.

Get past your pride and get into a position for God to work miraculously through you. Many have a high opinion of themselves, just as Naaman does. In your own mind you are a legend. A person may believe that God is privileged to have someone such as him or her in His service. Some have to get past their pride.

Get past your preconceptions. Some people have preconceptions about the Bible, the church, and the preacher. Humble yourself before Almighty God. Acknowledge that He, not you, is God and that His way will be your way. You will be getting into a position to see God move in a miraculous fashion in your life.

Obey Him fully. Partial obedience never will result in the full blessings of God. Some decide early that they simply will not do some things. They never will lower themselves to get relationships right in their lives. They will not obey God with their finances. They will dip twice, maybe three times, but seven times? Forget it. I simply will not do it, you say. To get your miracle, do what He says. You then will be in a position to be blessed beyond measure.

God still is in the miracle-working ministry today. Heroes, the high and mighty, the hypocrites, the haloes, and the healed still are among us today. He still uses them all to achieve His purposes. Get into a position for God's mighty working in your life.

Take a dip!

Chapter 12

WHEN THE IRON SWIMS

2 Kings 6:1-7

Elisha's ministry is one accompanied by several miracles that are somewhat low-profile when compared to the spectacular miracles of his mentor and predecessor, Elijah. The miracle under consideration in this passage is one of those done in an out-of-the-way situation that does not draw headlines or attention. It is done in connection with a group called "the company of the prophets." The King James Version calls it "the school of the prophets." This movement develops out of a crisis in the prophet Elisha's life. After that great spiritual renewal on Mt. Carmel when a contest between the gods occurs, Elisha spearheads a tremendous revival. He then falls into deep depression because of the pressure of his life and the loneliness that racks his soul. He believes he is all alone in the battle. All who serve Christ need encouragement and friendship in order to face the consistent battle that rages around us. Always be mindful that we are in a battle. The spoil is the souls of men.

"Finally, be strong in the Lord and in his mighty power. Put on the full armor of God so that you can take your stand against the devil's schemes. For our struggle is not against flesh and blood, but against the rulers, against the authorities, against the powers of this dark world and against the spiritual forces of evil in the heavenly realm" (Eph. 6:10-12).

Elisha needs support to help him stand in the throes of spiritual warfare. When we are alone, we are vulnerable. The school of the prophets originates to provide that network of support and encouragement for God's prophets.

These men begin to spend a lot of time together. Though they have other lives, they live in the same place and minister together and encourage each other and learn from each other. You might say it becomes the first seminary. This school of the prophets is in session on the day the iron did swim.

"The company of the prophets said to Elisha, 'Look, the place where we meet with you is too small for us. Let us go to the Jordan, where each of us can get a pole; and let us build a place there for us to live.' And he said, 'Go.' Then one of them said, 'Won't you please come with your servants?' 'I will,' Elisha replied. And he went with them. They went to the Jordan and began to cut down trees. As one of them was cutting down a tree, the iron axhead fell into the water. 'Oh, my lord,' he cried out, 'it was borrowed!' The man of God asked, 'Where did it fall?' When he showed him the place, Elisha cut a stick and threw it there, and made the iron float.

"Lift it out,' he said. Then the man reached out his hand and took it" (2 Kings 6:1-7).

The King James Version describes this moment as a time when "the iron did swim." Has such a day occurred in your life when the iron did swim? We can make some comparisons regarding the lost axhead and the loss of the joy of our salvation. They are amazing parallels.

THE DAY WHEN THE IRON DID SWIM

On this day when the iron did swim is a recognized desire. The school of the prophets is growing. Its members notice that where they are living has become quite crowded. To enhance their lives and ministry, one catches a vision to relocate. They put together a building committee, pray about it, talk about it, and bring it back to the group. They all agree: the school of the prophets needs a new campus. This new campus will provide additional space for greater ministry and growth. With unanimity they begin the project.

Change is inevitable if growth is occurring. If something is stagnant, no change is required. Anything that is growing is changing. We purchased a computer for our son to take to college. The salesperson assured us that this computer was top of the line—the fastest one available. As we drove home, I noticed a billboard announcing a new line of the same computer brand that made all the others, including the one we just purchased, obsolete!

Some new methods are appropriate to reach a new generation of people. Though the message of the Cross must remain central in our preaching and teaching, we cannot expect to reach the people of the 21st Century using methods that were effective in previous decades. The well-known parable states that the last seven words of the dying church are "we've never done it that way before!" Change is not good simply for change's sake. However, if growth occurs on a consistent basis, God-directed and Christ-centered change is required. The change always is in regard to the method, never the message.

Someone has the vision. Visionaries are necessary in the spiritual battle we face. Not only are visionaries needed, someone has to step up to do the work! Someone gets busy completing the vision with a responsible deed. Other options exist for the prophets. They could reason that since they are all men of prayer, they can pray and ask God to give them a new place. I believe in prayer, but I also believe a time arrives to work. For this school of the prophets, time has arrived to go to work in order to bring the vision into reality. Joshua learns this great truth in relation to the experience with Achan, who violates God's command during the conquest of Jericho. Joshua is face-down, stretched out before the Lord in prayer over his army's defeat at the small city of Ai.

"The Lord said to Joshua, 'Stand up! What are you doing on your face? Israel has sinned . . .' (Josh. 7:10-11a).

The time to pray has ended. The time has arrived for Joshua to rise from his knees, get to his feet, and rectify the situation. Recently one of the women in my church shared with me about a situation facing one of our members. She told me of the advice she had given, "Praying all the time is easy, but a point arrives when you've prayed enough. You need to go do something." A time arrives when we need to go to work.

Not long ago I learned a powerful truth packaged in a short phrase. That little phrase suggests that to become the person you wish to become, do the thing you do not want to do. Sometimes what we do not want to do is to go work for the Lord and just expect Him to do it all! Please understand: I realize that God works through us, yet our presence and effort still is required! I am sure that these prophets would rather have been preaching to the crowds than chopping the trees. But in order to become all God wanted them to become, they must do the thing they had rather not do.

Paul recognized that God blesses work.

"What, after all, is Apollos? And what is Paul? Only servants, through whom you came to believe as the Lord assigned to each his task. I planted the seed, Apollos watered it, but God made it grow" (1 Cor. 3:5-6).

To complete a task, do the work. Work is required to plant and to water. God is working through it all to bring in the harvest. In one of my churches a retired pastor enjoyed a fruitful ministry. I asked him his secret key to growing a church. His response was so simple. He said, "The people had a mind to work, and God blessed." God has allowed me to serve as the pastor of wonderful churches. In every context—rural, downtown, and suburban—we have experienced God's blessings and have grown. Different methods were employed at each church. At one of those churches, I personally knocked on the door of every home in the town and area. I really did not want to do that. Doing it was a lot of work. Yet to be what God wanted, I had to do what I had rather not do. The common denominator in all these ministries that resulted in God's blessings was diligent work!

I heard of a lost man that knocked on the door of the church. A man met him at the door and informed him that he could not help him. A seminar on soul-winning was conducted inside! A time arrives for us to get off our knees and get on our feet. It's time for us to get to work!

Whenever a work begins, a related dilemma will appear. As one of the prophets works, chopping down a tree, the axhead falls off and sinks into the Jordan River. An axhead in those days is a very expensive piece of equipment. These prophets have no money. The ax has been borrowed. The only way this prophet can repay the owner is to submit to him as a slave. The prophet is in a dilemma. He can continue to work. Even though the axhead is gone, he can keep chopping away, making a lot of noise, and wearing himself out. Although difficult work is required in the Lord's service, so is a sharp axhead. Working without the axhead may make a lot of noise, keep you busy and exhaust you, but not much will be accomplished.

When God begins to bless the vision and the work toward that vision, problems always will become evident. Almost all members of any church will tell you that they want the church to grow and to reach people for Christ. Often what they mean is that they are glad for growth if that does not challenge their comfort zone. In most cases, when a church begins to grow, the first objections that must be overcome are those from within the church. Very few growing churches have to face the wrath of a godless world which they begin to impact. Yet many have had to face the wrath of their own members who fought against change and the way things have always been. Once the challenge from within is conquered, wonderful problems regarding space, parking, and other challenges are good ones to face.

The lost axhead results in a restored delight. This young prophet shares with Elisha his dilemma. Understanding his character, Elisha probably mutters under his breath, "Boy, I don't know if you will ever make it as a prophet!" The young man shows him the place where the axhead sank, Elisha drops in a stick; the axhead surfaces. Some people will try to take the miraculous out of the Bible. They claim Elisha fishes around for the axhead, finds it, and pulls it out. What really happens is that the iron axhead miraculously floats to the surface of the water. That is not a big deal for our God. He can forgive sins and give eternal life. Floating an axhead is child's play for Him. As the young prophet reaches to take the axhead, relief and joy consume him. What is lost is found. He is delivered from becoming a slave to the owner of the axe.

When something of value that has been lost is found, it is a delight. If any of us would desire to bring joy and delight to the heart of our Master, we can involve ourselves in ministries and activities that bring lost people to a saving knowledge of Jesus Christ. When that is the focus of our lives, God will tax the farthest star to supply our needs to be successful in that work. That work is a delight.

THE DAY WHEN THE IRON SWIMS AGAIN

On the day when the iron swims again, a realized desire appears. Everyone shares the same basic desires. We have a desire to be forgiven. We have a desire to have our guilt taken away. We have a desire to have good relationships in our lives and to be joyful in our homes, to be fulfilled in our careers, to have a purpose in our life. The only way the basic desires of our lives can be fulfilled is in Jesus Christ. The moment one acknowledges Jesus Christ as Lord, forgiveness immediately is granted and experienced. The guilt, shame, remorse, and failure that you carry around in your suitcase is taken away. It has been nailed to the cross. You have a new touch in your heart. It's the Holy Spirit living within you. You have the assurance that your name now is written in God's Book; you have been given eternal life, and your heart is filled with joy. For you, that was the day the iron did swim. Do you remember that? It was awesome. Usually God gives us a vision—a dream for our lives. It is a vision for ministry— for life. Revisit that moment and that dream God gave you. All our desires are realized through a personal relationship with the Lord Jesus Christ.

Following Jesus Christ as a disciple is how these desires and dreams are realized. Through a responsible deed you take the first steps toward your dream. You become an ambassador of Jesus Christ. You begin to realize that everywhere you go, you represent the kingdom of God. Your desire at work, recreation, school, and at home is to be a responsible follower of Jesus Christ.

The ministries of the church are perfectly and beautifully designed to assist you to fulfill this God-given dream for your life. The fellowship provides friendship, support, and encouragement. The worship, both private and corporate, provides opportunities to stay connected to the power source of our lives and to keep our fellowship with our Savior dynamic and alive. The evangelism aspect offers opportunities to tell others about Christ. The discipleship aspect helps you grow in your faith. The ministry aspect offers you opportunities to use your God-given gifts to bless others and assists you to sharpen, define, and fulfill you dream. When you remain connected through those five aspects of church ministry, you will remain sharp; the axhead remains attached. The joy keeps flowing in your life. Your life becomes effective in the hands of the Master.

During this process, a related dilemma often occurs. As you seek to fulfill that God-given vision and the destiny God has for you, you can lose your joy. The axhead—the joy—somehow releases from your life. Many who still serve Christ have lost their joy. They have lost the axhead. The axhead is lost while the prophet is working. This doesn't happen because he is lazy. His intentions always are good. Followers of Christ, as incredible as it seems, can lose the joy of their salvation even while they are at work for the Lord. You can lose the joy as you preach, teach, sing, serve, and witness.

Many continue to serve without the joy. Week by week, as a pastor, I can see them in the congregation. They are not present to worship and honor the King of Kings; they are present because Sunday is the day they go to church. Those who continue to serve without the joy of the Lord often continue to chop at trees without a sharp axhead—just an axhandle. Lots of noise you hear, but never does a tree fall. If you listen closely, every Sunday you can hear the sound of people banging on trees with only the axhandle. They are in Bible-study classes and in choirs and praise teams, standing at the door as an usher and sitting in a pew with an eye on their watches. They have lost the joy of their salvation. They need the iron to swim again in their lives.

The great news is that the joy of our Lord's salvation can be restored. When that happens, it is a restored delight. For this to happen, realize that the joy is missing. The Bible tells us that the joy of the Lord is our strength. Jesus Christ tells us that He has come that your joy might be full. The angels announce the birth of Jesus Christ with the pronouncement, "Joy to the world, the Lord has come."

Realize the joy is missing. Only you really can answer that. No longer does singing praise in corporate worship light up your soul. Attendance at worship is optional. Ministry has become such a burden that you no longer are involved. The Bible remains on the shelf except for Sundays. You have the form down for cutting trees; you just have lost the axhead. Even though it is gone, you still hack away but get nothing done.

Secondly, realize that it is borrowed. It is a joy God Himself has given us. It is not a joy that depends on anything in our lives. You can be undergoing the most intense trial and hardships and difficulties that you could imagine and still be overwhelmed with the joy of the Lord. It is not your joy; you can't get it from doing something. It's the joy of the Lord. It is His to give.

To get it back, remember from whence you received it. You received it from knowing Jesus Christ and being overwhelmed in His presence. If the iron ever did swim the first time in your life, remember it was His. Even though you have lost it, He stands ready to give it back.

To get the joy back and recover the lost axhead, remember where you lost it. Perhaps it was some small thing with which you refused to deal. You may have gotten careless in your prayer time and in your personal time alone with God and His Word. Perhaps you allowed other interests to take precedence over your quest to accomplish God's dream for your life. You got sidetracked by the worries of this life, the deceit of riches, and the desires for other things. Maybe you got disconnected from the church and dropped out for while. Your spirit has dried up. Perhaps someone injured you or disappointed you. Perhaps you have become involved in a relationship or lifestyle that you know is not consistent with the lifestyle of a disciple of the Lord Jesus Christ. You can lose the joy in so many ways, but remember where you lost it.

Finally, receive it back. When this young prophet does what the old prophet says, he gets the axhead back. This simply involves going back where he lost it, then reaching down and picking it up. Sounds easy enough, doesn't it? He has to listen to Elisha to restore the axhead.

Pay attention to what is said from the pulpit of your church; follow the directions God gives through His man. God truly speaks to us all; the ground truly is level at the foot of the Cross. Also true is that not many, if any, have pored over and prayed over and received a message from God to speak to the people as much as has the prophet God has placed in the pulpit. Many who have lost their joy continue to beat on the trees week after week after week and hear sermon after sermon after sermon but do not really ever listen to even one.

If you really desire the joy of Jesus Christ back in your life, and you really desire for the iron to swim again, bury your pride and discover where you lost it. Every day I make my prayer this prayer of the psalms. David asks God to restore the joy of His salvation. He loses it through his adulterous affair with Bathsheba. He knows where he has lost it. He goes back to that place to retrieve it.

"Create in me a pure heart, O God, and renew a steadfast spirit within me. Do not cast me from your presence or take your Holy Spirit away from me. Restore to me the joy of your salvation and grant me a willing spirit, to sustain me. Then I will teach transgressors your ways, and sinners will turn back to you" (Ps. 51:10-13).

A connection exists among purity, repentance, and joy before one has effective ministry. Go back to the place you lost your joy. Ask God to restore the joy of His great salvation.

During seminary days a friend of mine had tremendous joy and enthusiasm about knowing Jesus Christ. I so much enjoyed being around him. One day there another seminarian visited with us. After my joyful friend left, the other seminarian commented, "I can remember when I had that kind of joy. It won't last. He will get over it." I replied, "I pray to God that I never get over it!"

Have you gotten over it? Perhaps this is the day that the iron swims again in your life.

Chapter 13

OPENED EYES

2 Kings 6:8-17

Has this ever occurred with you? You open the refrigerator door in search for ketchup. You simply cannot find it. In my case, I ask my wife if we have any. "Yes, it's in the door", is her answer, to which I reply, "I'm looking in the door. It's not here." She rounds the corner, reaches into the door, and hands me a nice bottle of ketchup. "Jim, open your eyes. It is right in front of you." A man in this chapter of God's Word needed to open his eyes. Glorious things were around him. May our prayer and desire be that God will give us opened eyes.

"Now the king of Aram was at war with Israel. After conferring with his officers, he said, 'I will set up my camp in such and such a place.' The man of God sent word to the king of Israel: 'Beware of passing that place, because the Arameans are going down there.' So the king of Israel checked on the place indicated by the man of God. Time and again Elisha warned the king, so that he was on his guard in such places. This enraged the king of Aram. He summoned his officers and demanded of them, 'Will you not tell me which of us is on the side of the king of Israel?' 'None of us, my lord the king,' said one of his officers, 'but Elisha, the prophet who is in Israel, tells the king of Israel the very words you speak in your bedroom.' 'Go find out where he is,' the king ordered, 'so I can send men and capture him.' The report came back: 'He is in Dothan.' Then he sent horses and chariots and a strong force there. They went by night and surrounded the city. When the servant of the man of God got up and went out early the next morning, an army with horses and chariots had surrounded the city. 'Oh, my lord, what shall we do?' the servant asked. 'Don't be afraid,' the prophet answered. 'Those who are with us are more than those who are with them.' And Elisha prayed, 'O Lord, open his eyes so he may see.' Then the Lord opened the servant's eyes, and he looked and saw the hills full of horses and chariots of fire all around Elisha (2 Kings 6:8-17).

The passage goes on to tell how Elisha prays and how the army is blinded before being led into the city of Samaria. When the soldiers receive back their sight, the king of Israel wants to kill them. Elisha advises to feed them and send them home, which they do. The Bible says that raiding parties from Aram do not enter Israel's territory again.

Ponder Elisha's prayer, "Lord, open his eyes." Often when a conversation takes a spiritual twist, many have absolutely no clue about the topic. When I talk to our computer expert at our church, he speaks a language with which I am unfamiliar. My eyes gloss over; I don't have a clue. When considering spiritual truth, things always have been that way. Things were that way in the Apostle Paul's day also.

"The man without the Spirit does not accept the things that come from the Spirit of God, for they are foolishness to him, and he cannot understand them, because they are spiritually discerned" (1 Cor. 2:14).

Even when speaking to gatherings of people who claim to know Christ, I've seen blank stares in the audience when I mention topics such as living by faith and trusting the hand

and will of God in all situations. The listeners seem blind to spiritual truth. The media outlets in our land today have no clue what people of faith are about. They view us as intellectual illiterates bordering on the superstitious. They simply are unable to understand spiritual truth. It is all foolishness to them. Let's join in Elisha's prayer, "Lord, open their eyes."

A SECRET PROCLAIMED

The King of Aram is being frustrated. A leak in his council has occurred. He is told, it's not us, it's the preacher! Now Elisha gets the blame for a lot of stuff, as most preachers do, but this time it is correct. He is revealing secrets. He is getting a word from God and passing it on. Secrets have a way of being found out. No one gets away with anything. Consider these passages:

"Do not revile the king even in your thoughts, or curse the rich in your bedroom, because a bird of the air may carry your words, and a bird on the wing may report what you say" (Eccl. 10:20).

"For there is nothing hidden that will not be disclosed, and nothing concealed that will not be known or brought out into the open" (Luke 8:17).

Something is mysterious about how God reveals the secrets of our lives. As they leave worship, members of our church have shared with me how God gave them insight, rebuke, or encouragement through the message. I stand amazed when I think about how the message had absolutely nothing to do with their topic of concern. God was at work proclaiming secrets!

When you think of secrets proclaimed, remember that absolutely nothing has escaped the notice of our God. He knows what we have stuffed away in secret places, the bitterness we have tucked away in our heart, and the plans we have that might injure someone. He has heard every word we have ever spoken—even every thought that we have not spoken. You may think that you have a secret. You really don't.

A SPECIAL PRAYER

Not only is Elisha revealing secrets, he also wants to share one. Elisha wants to share this secret with his servant. That is when he makes this special prayer, "O Lord, open his eyes so that he may see."

This is truly a great compliment to Elisha. An entire army is sent against one man. I mean, he's just one man. Why do you need to send an army to get one man? We have armies looking for terrorists, but they have supporters around them. Elisha is just one man not in hiding; an army is required to attempt to capture him. I was told that years, even centuries ago, a great leader with his army received a report that said, "We are outnumbered. We've counted us and counted them. We're highly outnumbered." The leader said, "How many did you count for me?" I think of an occasion when soldiers were ordered to arrest Jesus Christ. They returned without Him to those who sent them. When asked why they did not arrest Him, they replied that no one ever spoke like Him. They did not desire to lay a hand on Him.

Perhaps this army has heard about what Elisha has done with Naaman. Perhaps others of his exploits have been told. Interestingly the enemies of Israel have greater regard for the man of God than do the prophet's own people. The king of Aram realizes Elisha is more than a mere man. He realizes a powerful, mighty God stands with him. So an army of footmen, an army of cavalry, and an army of chariots arrive to arrest against one man. He is armed with a sword, which is the Word of God. He is armed with a breastplate of righteousness. He is armed with the shield of faith and a helmet of salvation. That's all he has; that's all he needs. We have the same weapons. Let's wear them.

A great concern also is present. The greatest prayer always rises out of the greatest concern. We really begin to seek God's face in prayer when the great challenge or season of adversity arrives in our lives. This servant knows that Elisha has been tipping off the king of Israel. He also knows why the army is there. Elisha has enemies in high places. You can tell how great a person is by who his enemies are. For the servant, the day of reckoning has arrived. The servant is thinking that if they get Elisha, they will get him as well. His question to Elisha, "O, my Lord, what shall we do?" Better understood, "How can we save our lives?"

He is not even aware of his own blindness. On one occasion, after the Lord Jesus has healed a blind man, the Pharisees ask if they are blind as well. When someone is physically blind, that person knows it. When one is spiritually blind, that person has no idea, until perhaps, a great concern enters his or her life.

Open your eyes in several areas—not the least of which is for our eyes to be open to our enemy. Our enemy is none other than Satan himself. He is a scary, frightening being. His only goal is to hurt and defeat our God. He hurts what God loves the most—His people. His goal is to kill, steal, and destroy. He is very good at what he does. He is destroying lives in record numbers. He is a deceiver and a schemer. He gets people in a position where they do not see any danger in what he is doing in their lives. I never cease to be amazed at how some parents can be blinded to the things they are allowing in their kids—things that will absolutely devastate their children's lives. Thinking no harm, no foul, and that kids will be kids, rather than opening their eyes to the enemy, they allow their children to open their lives to the dangers of temptation and to the evil and destruction that sin always brings.

The numbers of those blinded to our enemy are staggering. If you have given your life to Jesus Christ, the enemy has lost your soul. At that point his strategy changes. He desires to render your witness ineffective so you will have little impact on anyone else's soul. Many stumble through life unfulfilled. They have little contentment and have manifold problems with relationships. They never even imagine that they have become a target of Satan, who is stealing their joy.

The great news for us, and Satan knows it, is that "those who are with us are more than those who are with them." Lord, open our eyes to our enemy.

Open your eyes to Jesus Christ as Lord. Many have different ideas on how they plan on getting into heaven. Some stand on religion. Their names are somewhere on a church roll; on occasion they attend a church. They believe that if they are inside a church building every now and again, their way to heaven is sure. I suppose they also believe that if they climbed into an oven, they would become a biscuit. Some stand on family. Their family had in it a grandfather who was a preacher. For those depending on that old preacher, a huge disappointment will arrive for you and for him. His faith is good for him only; his disappointment will be great when you miss heaven, because you are depending on his faith. Some stand on a good life. They believe they are not nearly as bad as some people they know. However, to gain entrance into heaven, you must be perfect. That ruins that position.

The bottom line is that only one way to heaven exists. Only God can open anyone's eyes to understand. That way is through a personal relationship with God's Son, Jesus Christ. In much of our theology of the day, we have lost a crucial aspect of that relationship. It is the lordship part. Too many would say yes to Christ as their ticket to heaven but no to His claim of lordship on their lives. I am not equipped to make a judgment call on anyone but myself, but I fear many will be eternally disappointed on the day they stand before Jesus Christ and realize that they did not really know Him at all. We pray: Lord, open our eyes to Jesus Christ as Lord.

Open your eyes to the Bible as truth. It speaks volumes about American Christianity when a plea from our hearts is that God might open the eyes of those who are called by His name to understand that the Bible is the truth of God. Pastors, churches, and denominations have walked away from the understanding that the Bible is the Word of God and that it is unchanging, objective, and eternal. We do not need to hear how someone interprets the Bible; we need to hear what the Bible says.

Both the Old and New Testaments have been inspired by the Spirit of God through special revelation which prevented any error in the original manuscripts. This is absolute truth on which we stake our eternity and can build our lives. Some people need to have their eyes opened to the Bible as truth. A truthful God that deals with His people with integrity would never give them a Word about Himself that changes with each generation. Based on God's character alone, the Bible is a perfect, accurate word on God, humanity, sin, heaven, hell, life, and morality. Lord, open our eyes to the Bible as truth.

Open your eyes to living in the Spirit. When someone experiences the Holy Spirit of God working in his or her life, it becomes one of those "ah-ha" moments! You never will be the same when you actually experience the Holy Spirit of God working through you. This makes such an impact that many mistakenly refer to this as a "second blessing", with Jesus Christ being the first blessing. The Bible disputes this theology, but the wonderful life in the Spirit really cannot be explained, only experienced.

"Praise be to the God and Father of our Lord Jesus Christ, who has blessed us in the heavenly realms with every spiritual blessing in Christ" (Eph. 1:3).

"His divine power has given us everything we need for life and godliness through our knowledge of him (Jesus Christ) who called us by his own glory and goodness" (2 Pet. 1:3).

Notice that in both passages, we already have received every spiritual blessing that exists, which includes all we need for life and godliness in Jesus Christ. When we enter into a relationship with Jesus Christ, we get all of God that is available to get. Our challenge becomes learning how to appropriate the gift we have received. This occurs by faith and by dying to ourselves. If we are filled with our ambition, goals, and dreams, we cannot be filled with the Holy Spirit. By faith empty yourself, so that He can fill you with Himself.

One day one of the senior saints at a church where I was the pastor arrived in my study. She said she had lived her entire life involved in church and never had heard anything such as what I had been sharing on the Spirit-filled life. She said this information was one of the most wonderful things she had ever heard as a follower of Christ. I'm not sure it had not been taught in any church where she had been. She simply had been blinded to this glorious truth until God opened her eyes. Lord, open our eyes to living in the Spirit.

We ask God to open our eyes to reduce our fear. We live in a scary world. Terrorists and terrorist threats are not really new. When I was a small child, drills were conducted so we would be prepared in the case of a nuclear attack. We were instructed to get under our desks. I often wondered how getting under my desk would protect me from an atomic bomb.

Some parents had trouble with their young son. Every morning they awoke to find him in the bed with them. The dad had a long talk with his little boy and told him that he must remain in his own bed all night. He assured the son that he had no reason to fear. That next night as the parents were about to fall asleep, the dad heard his boy call from his bedroom, "Daddy, is your face toward me?" The dad replied, "Yes, my face is toward you." The little boy's fear was gone. He was confident that his father's face was toward him. We have plenty of things that can frighten us. Recall again the words of the great prophet, "those who are with us are more than those who are with them." God's face is turned toward us. Lord, open our eyes to reduce our fear.

A SUPERNATURAL PRESENCE

When you study the life of Elisha, you can discover when his eyes are opened. In 2 Kings 1 and 2 he has seen his mentor call down fire from heaven when groups of 50 soldiers arrive to arrest him. He is an eyewitness to Elijah's being taken into God's presence in a whirlwind. This event gives him an even clearer focus. This allows him to walk in the confidence of a supernatural presence around his life. Don't underestimate the value of a mentor in your life. Likewise, don't underestimate the value of an apprentice. Eyes are opened in that process.

I am not certain that Elisha literally can see the hills full of horses and chariots of fire around him, but he knows they are there. The servant is not yet able to live by faith; he needs to actually see them. Once he sees them, I feel certain he never doubts their presence again. No way exists that anyone in that army will lay a hand on Elisha unless the Commander of the Chariots of Fire allows it. When any one of us makes an authentic run at serving the living God, the chariots of fire protect us. When that pastor stands in that pulpit to proclaim the Word of God, he is surrounded by chariots of fire. You might not see them, but they are there. "Those who are with us are more than those who are with them." The Apostle John writes of the same truth:

"You, dear children, are from God and have overcome them, because the one who is in you is greater than the one who is in the world" (1 John 4:4).

When one considers this supernatural presence, he or she needs to draw a conclusion. The one who is in the world does have power. This is a real army. Its members have sharp swords and spears. They have a foul attitude; they are dangerous. I do not wish to diminish any challenge you have in your life. Health concerns are real. Nothing can wrench the soul as much as financial crises with no clear way out. When parents deal with wayward children, they are looking for those chariots of fire. Issues that our students face regarding peer pressure and moral choices are as real and dangerous as is the army challenging Elisha. But when God opens your eyes, you can draw a comparison. Compared to the awesomeness of Almighty God, the king of Aram becomes a tin solder. Members of his army become toy soldiers when compared to the chariots of fire.

If only God would open our eyes to the glory of Jesus Christ, that challenge in our lives today would bow before the chariots of fire. As Peter walks on the water for that brief moment, he begins to sink when he takes his eyes off Jesus Christ. He does not realize that the waves that threatens to fall in over his head already are under the feet of the Lord Jesus.

The servant of Elisha has his focus taken away from the armies of Aram when his eyes are opened to the chariots of fire.

    The chariots of fire surround you now. Don't you see them? Lord, open our eyes.

Chapter 14

A LIVING LEGACY

2 Kings 13:20-21

Great servants of God enter and exit, while the work of God continues until Jesus returns. This text describes ever so briefly the end of an era. Another prophet with such influence and power as Elijah and Elisha will not appear again in Israel until John the Baptist. They are men who can call down the fire of God. Because of the lives and ministries of Elijah and Elisha, we are forever blessed. They leave all of us a tremendous legacy.

They both are great men of God, yet they are very different. Elijah dwells alone for the most part of his life, but when he shows up, thunder and fire occur. He burns everybody near him. He asks for no help, gives no quarter, and speaks of the judgment of God without tact or care of whom he offends. His only desire is to please his God. A chariot of God fittingly takes him to heaven. Elisha, on the other hand, is among the people. He usually works his miracles in the home. He is somewhat tenderhearted. He is at ease among the intelligentsia and royalty as well as among the common people. He nurtures the young prophets. But when necessary, he calls down the fire of heaven. He now is old—probably between 80 and 100 years of age, and dying of an old man's disease. As an old man, the grand power of God still flashes from him.

The incident before us is God's stamp of approval and authenticity on the life and legacy of Elisha. It is a living legacy.

Elisha dies and is buried. Moabite raiders enter the country every spring. Once while some Israelites are burying a man, suddenly they see a band of raiders, so they throw the man's body into Elisha's tomb. When the body touches Elisha's bones, the man springs to life and stands up on his feet (2 Kings 13:20-21).

What an event! What a surprise! The question would have to be asked, "Whose tomb is that? Whose bones are those?" The answer arrives, "Those are the bones of a prophet of God." Elijah and Elisha are men whose lives and ministries are marked by fire and by power and though being long departed from this earth, they still speak. They leave us a living legacy. That legacy impacts us, inspires us, and encourages us. Their lives paint their legacies, and once painted, they cannot be changed.

All of us receive a legacy. Some people in your life have invested in you and have left their mark on your life. Sometimes the legacies passed to us are tremendous and encouraging, as the legacies of these two great prophets are. Other times the legacies are negative and can haunt and destroy our lives. Many men have received a legacy of absenteeism from their father, or the legacy of a lifestyle that did not honor God. They live in the light of that legacy and pass the same kind to their children. They carry on a family tradition that fails to bring joy and meaning—only heartache and destruction.

None of us can control the legacy that we receive, but we do control the legacy we pass to those who follow us. Those who have received a positive, Christ-centered legacy honor those who left it to you by sending that same message with your legacy. Those who are recipients of a negative, hurtful legacy can see that the baton stops with them.

Several thoughts spring from this closing passage of Scripture about the legacy of Elisha. They center on the challenge of a living legacy.

PURPOSES THAT ARE DIVINE

Elisha is about to die. In 2 Kings 13:14-19, the king, Jehoash, visits him. Even though he is an evil king, Joash recognizes the value of this man of God and recognizes that when this man of God is gone, no one is on the horizon to step into that place. He expresses a personal inclination, which is so common to us all when a great person passes from life. That personal inclination is to ask the question, "What will we do now?" The anchor is gone. The great connection with God is gone. They had Elijah and then Elisha, but now they do not have another. We feel that way when the patriarch or the matriarch of the family dies and when a great person of God dies.

A reminder: who does the work really doesn't matter. What matters is that the work is done. In light of the personal inclination, we have a privileged implication. Holding Elisha in the highest regard, we recognize that God does not need him to get His work done. He does not need any of us. For any of us to be given the opportunity to serve God and join Him in His work is one of the most glorious and awesome privileges that can be afforded to humankind. He does not need us but allows us to get in on the work. Never lose the awe and wonder of the incredible blessing God has given us to walk alongside Him.

One of the great heroes of Southern Baptist life once said that if he had 1,000 lives to live, he would live every one of them as a preacher of the gospel of Jesus Christ. I join him in that assessment. I cannot possibly describe in any fitting terms the unspeakable, holy privilege I have to preach the gospel. Any person is no less privileged than I am to serve our God in whatever manner He directs, whether teaching a Bible class, singing in a praise team, or setting up tables. Being involved in God's work is a privilege. His purposes for us are divine. None of us may be able to call down the fire, but we can do our part. The work goes on; to share in it indeed is a blessing.

PROCESSES THAT ARE DETERMINED

Learn the mastery of a legacy. Leaving a legacy of life is a process. You paint your legacy as you live. Elisha's tomb probably is a small cave, cut out in the rock, and covered by a large rock, much like the tomb of the Lord Jesus Christ. In a hurry to bury a friend, these men remove the outer rock and lay the man inside Elisha's burial vault. The dead man gets up and walked out with them! He has touched a legacy of life. He has touched Elisha's bones. Jesus taught that God is not the God of the dead but of the living. Elisha has mastered his legacy. He pictures for us the thought of the writer of Hebrews.

"And by faith he still speaks, even though he is dead" (Heb. 11:4).

Elisha's legacy still speaks, even though he has been dead for a long time. His life determines his legacy. His legacy will not have been one of life had his life not so ordered.

In the process of God's working through your life, a legacy is developed. Don't expect to leave a positive, encouraging legacy unless you are living the life. Years ago, in a small town, a man was known as the town gambler and drunk. He beat his wife and abused his kids. Everybody in the town knew him well. When he died, his brother offered $5,000 to any preacher who at the funeral would say that his brother had been a saint. The Baptist preacher agreed. At the funeral, with a packed house, the pastor said, "We all know the kind of life this man lived. He was a drunkard and abused his wife and children. He gambled away everything he ever had, but compared to his brother, he was a saint!" The legacy you will leave is the life you are living right now. Do not expect the legacy to be mastered if it does not match the life.

The legacy also has a mystery. Sometimes you never know what your legacy might really mean. Dr. W. A. Criswell was the beloved pastor of the First Baptist Church of Dallas, Texas, for more than half a century. I attended his funeral and never have attended a church meeting as powerful and meaningful as that one. His legacy is clear and easy to determine. His life was large, as is his legacy.

Not everyone's legacy is so clear-cut. Sometimes, we may be leaving a legacy that no one even knows we left. Our senior adults traveled through the little town where I served my first pastorate. The church brought the sandwiches for our group. We ate at the church and had a worship service. As I sat across the table from one of the men at that church, we talked a little bit. I spent more than two years there. He looked at me at said, "You know, I'm trying my very best, but I just can't remember you." Ouch! Whether he remembers me doesn't matter. He was exposed to the Word of God through my preaching; that was an investment in his life. He received part of my legacy and does not even know it, but God does. As we serve Christ, we are passing things into people's lives. They are legacies that God will never forget.

A family in Jerusalem during Jeremiah's ministry leaves a legacy like that. The patriarch of the family is a man named Jonadab, son of Recab. His clan is known as the Recabites. The legacy they receive from their forefather has been honored throughout the generations. Their commitment to honor the legacy handed to them is largely unnoticed by all, but not by God. Note the mystery of God's blessing on this family.

"Jonadab son of Recab will never fail to have a man to serve me" (Jer. 35:19).

Somewhere in our world today, 2,500 years later, probably unknowing, is a preacher serving God who, if possible, could trace his family lineage to Jonadab, son of Recab. He is serving God because God is honoring the legacy of this man.

Today this mystery of a legacy continues. You probably have some blessings in your life that are the result an unnamed, unknown ancestor of yours who took a stand for God; God honored that by blessing yet unborn generations. You may not know who to thank for it, but God does. It is the mystery of a legacy.

Our challenge is to paint our lives in such a way as to pass a blessing to our families. Should the Lord tarry another 2,000 years, we can desire that our families even thousands of years later will be blessed by the commitments we make today. Some descendants could be blessed immeasurably by the legacy we pass. As you live for Jesus Christ, you never know how far your influence will carry. It is a mystery—an awesome mystery.

PRACTICES THAT ARE DEVELOPED

The great question then becomes, how can I leave a legacy of life? You can do this through three steps. They are simple and obvious. The first is an authentic commitment to Jesus Christ as Savior and Lord. Leaving a powerful, positive, spiritual legacy to anybody apart from a commitment to Jesus Christ is impossible This commitment means that you recognize that only by the grace of God that are you forgiven. Only by the grace of God do you have an eternal home in heaven. Only by the grace of God are we able to live day by day for Him. Remember that God can do the work on His own, but He has in His sovereign will opened the door to give us the privilege to join Him in His great purposes.

The story is told of a man standing before the gates of heaven and requesting entrance. He is told he must have accumulated 1,000 points in his life to gain entrance. After inquiring how points were gained, the man exclaimed, "I'll only get in by the grace of God!" He then heard the exclamation, "Enter into the joy of your Master." Commitment to Jesus Christ, glorying in the grace, and walking in the Spirit will leave a legacy of life.

The second step is obedience to Jesus Christ. You cannot leave a legacy of life when your family members have observed you live in disobedience to God's will. Someone would have to pay a preacher off to say it at your funeral if you did not do it. When your family is facing a decision, the children need to hear you say, "We will do what God desires in this decision, because the primary focus for our lives is to be obedient in the will of God." When your children ask you why you are doing some task, tell them because you desire to be obedient to Jesus Christ. Those kinds of things will make lasting impressions on them that they will pass to future generations. You are painting for them a legacy that never will be erased. You cannot paint that legacy until you actually live it.

A third step in passing the legacy is participation in God's purposes. God has a place for you in the work. When you trusted Christ as savior, you were gifted. If you desire to pass a legacy that will be an encouragement and a blessing, find the place that fits you in the work of God through your local church. Can you imagine Elijah or Elisha having anything of a legacy had they not obeyed God's will for their life in ministry? They would just have been another name on another genealogical roll in Israel. But because they were participating in God's work, they still stand today passing down these living legacies to us. Seek, find, and fulfill God's purpose for your life by participating in that work. Make God's agenda more important than your agenda. Who knows? You may have a great-great-great-grandson one day who becomes the greatest minister of the Gospel the world has ever seen. That will happen because God is honoring a legacy that you left while you painted your life here. You will share in that reward.

The time to consider your legacy is now. Never expect anyone in your sphere of influence to live the life that you do not live. Live the life; paint the legacy as you go. You will be blessed. In the future when someone thinks about you, it will bring life to them.

The Apostle Paul writes his own legacy. This also could be said of Elijah and Elisha. I desire it to be true of me.

"I have fought the good fight, I have finished the race, I have kept the faith. Now there is in store for me the crown of righteousness, which the Lord, the righteous Judge, will award to me on that day—and not only to me, but also to all who have longed for his appearing" (2 Tim. 4:7-8).

Paul's legacy is one of life. He is faithful to the faith, faithful to the fight, and faithful to the finish. Elijah is also, as is Elisha. I plan to be. I hope you do as well.

Being faithful to the faith means that you honor and live by the ancient truths of the Bible. That body of Truth that defines our faith is held in high esteem. To be faithful to the fight means that you are involved in that spiritual warfare, battling all the forces of hell for the souls of people. To be faithful to the finish means that you have not and will not quit until God calls you home, whether it be in a chariot or from an old man's disease. To pass on a legacy of life, remain faithful in all three areas.

A pastor friend of mine had been diagnosed with cancer. On a regular basis I called to encourage him and to let him know I was praying for him. For a while he appeared to be beating that horrible disease. One day I received a call telling me that he had died. I did not realize that he had taken a sudden turn for the worse. The next week after his death I received his church newsletter and sat in stunned silence as I read words he had penned. I felt as though he were speaking to me from the grave:

"I never thought I would be writing from this perspective, but I am a terminal cancer patient. I have fought this with every resource available. Unless God chooses to do a miraculous healing, I will go to be with Him very soon, perhaps within days. Meanwhile, I am living day by day and trusting God's grace. I will continue serving Him and preaching with whatever life and strength He gives me until He calls me home.

"You have been a wonderful church. Thank you for all you have been to me. I will serve you with strength and love as God provides. I will serve you lovingly until God calls me home."

He still speaks, even though he is dead. He has left a legacy of life, faithful to the faith, to the fight, and to the finish. May we do nothing less.

The prophets who could call down the fire have left us their legacies. They arrived in Israel during desperate times, but now they are gone. Our times are no less desperate. How we need for God to raise up a generation of prophets who will call down the fire! With one voice may we ask God to send us men with the spirit of Elijah and Elisha, who once again can call down the fire!

Order more copies of
Calling Down the Fire
and obtain a free CrossHouse catalog
CALL: 1-800-747-0738
FAX: 1-888-252-3022
Email: crosshousepublishing@earthlink.net
Mail copy of form below to:
CrossHouse Publishing
P.O. Box 461592
Garland, Texas 75046
Visit: www.crosshousepublishing.com

Number of copies desired _____
Multiply number of copies by $9.95 ____X___$9.95___
Cost of books: $_____
Please add $3 for postage and handling for first book and add 50-cents for each additional book in the order.
Shipping $_____
Texas residents add 8.25 % sales tax $_____

Total order $_____

Check # enclosed _____
Credit card # _____ exp. date_____
  (Visa, MasterCard, Discover, American Express accepted)

Name _____

Address _____

City State, Zip _____

Phone _____ FAX _____

Email _____